What Mark's readers are saying

"I recently picked up a copy of your book. I'm only halfway through, but I already feel like it's one of the most important books I've ever held in my hands."

"A Major [in Iraq] shared a copy of your book with me. When I started to read it, I couldn't put it down. I've gotten several more copies and given them to subordinates and superiors."

"Your insight is amazing, your sense of humor delightful! Thank you for putting into words what was in my heart. I've read numerous books written by Christian authors, and none has ministered to my experience the way your book did."

"Your book satisfied me like water in the desert."

"Thank you so much for bringing the Lord's Word to me through your book. I am new to the church and am only starting to study the Bible. Your book gave me so much comfort and, most of all, hope."

"I purchased your book two weeks ago, and it has not left my side since. Thank you from the bottom of my heart for your inspiration."

"A good friend gave me your book and I couldn't put it down. I plan to read it again and again for reminders."

"I cannot tell you how your book has ministered to me. I ordered ten copies to pass out to my friends.

free refill

free
refill

coming back for more of Jesus

mark atteberry

Standard®
PUBLISHING
Bringing The Word to Life

Cincinnati, Ohio

Published by Standard Publishing, Cincinnati, Ohio
www.standardpub.com

Printed in the United States of America.
Project editor: Lynn Lusby Pratt
Cover and interior design: studiogearbox.com

Published in association with the literary agency of Alive Communications, Inc., 7680 Goddard St., Suite 200, Colorado Springs, Colorado, 80920.

ISBN 0-7847-1912-8

Library of Congress Cataloging-in-Publication Data
Atteberry, Mark.
    Free refill : coming back for more of Jesus / Mark Atteberry.
      p. cm.
    ISBN 0-7847-1912-8 (case bound)--ISBN 0-7847-7273-8 (perfect bound)
      1. Bible. N.T. Gospels–Criticism, interpretation, etc. 2. Faith–Biblical teaching. 3. Spirituality–Biblical teaching. I. Title.

  BS2555.6.F3A88 2007
  242.5--dc22   2006021964

13 12 11 10 09 08 07   9 8 7 6 5 4 3 2 1

contents

GOD GIVES FREE REFILLS

Emptiness.

If you want to understand the urgency it can cause, talk to someone who's just bitten into a red-hot jalapeño, has an empty iced tea glass, and can't find his waiter.

If you want to understand the frustration it can cause, talk to someone whose car just coughed and sputtered to a rolling stop because he forgot to gas it up.

If you want to understand the stress it can cause, talk to someone with an empty bank account who still has one bill left to pay.

And if you want to understand the pain it can cause, talk to someone who's just been burned for the umpteenth time by the empty promises of a faithless spouse.

Throughout our lives, we encounter the desolation known as emptiness. From the baby who sucks the last drop of formula out of his bottle, to the octogenarian who shakes his last blood pressure pill into his palm, we all fight a never-ending battle against dwindling supplies. And Christians have it even tougher than unbelievers when it comes to this battle because we not only have to deal with emptiness in all its standard configurations, we also have to deal with the thorny problem of dwindling faith.

Yes, I know faith isn't supposed to dwindle. Faith is supposed to grow. But this isn't a perfect world, and things don't always work out the way they're supposed to. It doesn't always snow on Christmas. The ideal couple doesn't always live happily ever after. The Cardinals don't always win the World Series. And Christians aren't always brimming with faith.

Perhaps you've noticed.

Maybe, even as you hold this book in your hands, you're experiencing your very own faith famine. Perhaps life has roughhoused you to the limit of your endurance and is now smirking and asking what you're going to do about it. You know you ought to be able to say or do something really spiritual and claim a mighty victory for the Lord, but all you can think of is curling up in the fetal position and hiding your eyes.

If you've ever had this experience, or are having it now, don't panic. I've got some good news for you.

YOU'RE NOT ALONE

It should comfort you to know that some of the greatest heroes of the Bible saw their faith dwindle to almost nothing. A striking example is John the Baptist.

He was a relative of Jesus, a pull-no-punches preacher who courageously challenged people to repent and clearly identified Jesus as the long-awaited Messiah. One day, he saw Jesus approaching and said, "Look! There is the Lamb of God who takes away the sin of the world!" (John 1:29). There wasn't a doubt in his mind that he was speaking the truth. He was brimming with faith.

But later, circumstances turned against him, and he found himself sitting in a prison cell. Suddenly, the truth didn't seem so cut and dried. Things he'd always believed didn't seem quite as certain. In fact, at one point he became so unsettled about his core beliefs that he sent a couple of his friends to find Jesus and ask him a pointed question: "Are you the Messiah we've been expecting, or should we keep looking for someone else?" (Luke 7:19). That question is a stunning reminder that even the staunchest followers of Christ occasionally need a faith refill.

So don't feel bad if *you* do. Don't listen to that little voice inside your head that keeps telling you what a pathetic excuse for a Christian you are. It's not true. What is true is that you're just like

John the Baptist and every other imperfect person trying to scratch out an existence in this fallen world. You are not alone.

But there's even more good news.

God Gives Free Refills

Jesus gave John's messengers a specific answer that holds the key to refilling any person's faith. He said: "Go back to John and tell him what you have seen and heard—the blind see, the lame walk, the lepers are cured, the deaf hear, the dead are raised to life, and the Good News is being preached to the poor" (Luke 7:22).

I love the fact that Jesus didn't respond to John's question by dragging out his sermon file. Just think of all the ancient messianic prophecies he could have quoted and expounded upon. But no, he understood that John needed a lifeline, not a lecture. So he threw him one. He urged John to look again at what he, Jesus, was accomplishing.

You're probably thinking, *But wait! It can't be that simple. There has to be more to replenishing a person's faith than that.* No, there isn't. If there were, Jesus would have said so. He would have laid out a detailed plan or itemized a list of requirements. There's no way he would have given his dear friend a flawed, incomplete answer, knowing it would doom him to further anxiety.

The good news is that nothing has changed. After all these years, faith refills are still free and can still be accomplished by focusing on Jesus. Hebrews 12:1, 2 says, "Let us run with endurance the race that God has set before us. *We do this by keeping our eyes on Jesus, on whom our faith depends from start to finish.*" (emphasis added)

The problem with most of us is that we want to overcomplicate this process. We assume that something as valuable as a faith refill ought to cost us something, so we try to acquire it through physical effort. We squeeze even more religious activities into our already overcrowded schedules. We restart our daily devotions (for the ten thousandth time). We run out and buy the latest Christian best seller and start highlighting it with a yellow marker. We hand our lunch money over to the dirty, bearded beggar holding the hand-scribbled cardboard sign at the intersection. And, of course, we recommit (again, for the ten thousandth time) to taming that nasty little habit we've managed to keep a secret for years.

But it never works.

It *never* works.

Because frenzied activity, even if it's well-intentioned, saps our strength and dulls our senses. It fills our lives, not with faith but with noise that drowns out his still, small voice. Worst of all, it makes us numb to his often-featherlike touch.

That's why I wrote this book.

I want to show you how to get a free refill. I want to take your hand, lead you away from the madhouse that is your life, and ask you to slow down and have an encounter with the one on whom your faith depends from start to finish.

Remember Mary and Martha? When Jesus came to visit, Martha fretted and fussed herself to a frazzle in the kitchen while Mary contentedly sat at his feet and got her faith topped off. Jesus himself remarked that Mary had discovered the one thing in life that is truly important (Luke 10:38-42).

My goal, then, is to draw you out of your kitchen (or office), away from your pots and pans (or your Palm Pilot and laptop), and park you at the feet of Jesus. I want you to see again what he did. I want you to hear again what he said. I want you to contemplate again the difference he makes in people's lives. And through it all, I want you to be reminded of why you fell in love with him in the first place.

When that happens . . . mark my word. You will be changed.

Your strength will be renewed.

Your passion will be rekindled.

Your joy will be restored.

And your faith will be refilled.

1
REFILLING YOUR FAITH IN HIS UNDERSTANDING

JOHN 4:5-30

The phrase "I've been there" is in the chorus of Christ's theme song.

—MAX LUCADO

I used to believe there were no magic words.

Oh sure, as a kid I would say "Open sesame!" or "Abracadabra!" when a childish game of make-believe called for a mysterious incantation. But I never took the words seriously and, truthfully, never knew what they meant. Still don't.

Later, when I was a young minister, troubled people would come to me looking for help with their thorny problems. If their expectations seemed a little too high, I found I could quickly temper them by saying, "Just remember . . . there aren't any magic words."

But I now realize I was wrong.

There are in fact two words that, when spoken together at just the right moment, have amazing, life-changing power. No, they're not magical in the Harry Potter, wand-waving sense. But make no mistake. These two words have been known to breathe new life into wheezing, withering souls. They've been known to lift burdens, calm fears, and inspire hope. Timed right, they are as refreshing as a cold front in July.

I'm referring to the words *I understand.*

Right behind food, shelter, and clothing, one of our greatest needs is to be understood. If you doubt this, think about what happens when you get into conflict with your spouse, your boss, or your children. Don't you find yourself constantly rehearsing speeches in your head? As you're driving, pumping gas, or lying in bed at night, don't you play out various scenarios in your mind and itemize all the clever things you plan to say the next time the issue is discussed? The reason you do this is because you can't stand thinking that the people you're butting heads with don't understand your point of view. You're determined to enlighten them if it's the last thing you do!

Or what happens when you're unfairly criticized? Don't you immediately start ranting about all the things your critic just doesn't understand?

Or how do you feel when you're lonely, depressed, or grieving and somebody tells you to snap out of it? Don't you instantly mark that person down as having no understanding of what you're going through? And doesn't that realization make you feel even more isolated?

But surely the most painful moment of all comes when you've committed a terrible sin and some Goody Two-shoes starts lecturing you. You know that person doesn't share your particular weakness and, therefore, doesn't understand what a struggle it is for you to keep yourself pure.

Think about it.

Many of our most frustrating moments come when we desperately need understanding and can't seem to find it. That's why the words *I understand* are so powerful. They're a lifeline to a drowning soul. Say them to someone who's hurting, confused, or neck deep in a messy situation, and just watch the reaction. At the very least, you'll see a sigh of relief. There's a good chance you'll get a hug. You might even see tears of joy. It feels wonderful to know that somebody understands.

But let me offer a warning:

Understanding cannot be faked.

If you tell someone you understand when you really don't, you'll come off looking as fake as a ten-dollar toupee. The words will lose all their power, and you'll lose all your credibility. And let's face it. There *are* going to be many people and situations you will *not* understand, because the world is full of gut-wrenching human dramas that defy logic.

This truth was driven home to me when our chief of police gave me a tour of the new multimillion dollar police station that opened in our city. We strolled through offices, conference rooms, labs, and staging areas. But when we walked into the vice department, something happened that I'll never forget.

The room was quite large and contained several workstations. Along one wall was a shelf that held dozens of thick, three-ring binders. I didn't notice them until the chief gestured in their direction and said, "Those notebooks contain records on all the women we've arrested for prostitution."

I looked at the books and back at the chief. "You can't be serious," I said.

Seeing an opportunity to enlighten a naive citizen, the chief walked over and pulled one of the notebooks off the shelf. He opened it at random and handed it to me. There, frozen in time, was the face of a sad-looking woman. She wasn't pretty, though I suspect she might have been at one time. Her hair was in disarray, and she wore no makeup, which somehow surprised me. Her eyelids drooped. She looked run-down and used up.

I turned the pages and saw other faces, equally worn out and desperate—women who no doubt had once gone to church, played with Barbie dolls, harbored secret schoolgirl crushes, and attended senior proms with nervous, pimply, teenage boys. What on earth had happened to them? In a land of opportunity and at a time when women are freer than ever to soar, why did they choose a lifestyle that promised nothing but a crash?

I have no idea.

Neither do you.

And that's the point.

There are unfathomable human mysteries all around us. There are people whose choices have been so bad and whose lives have become so hopelessly tangled that anyone who claimed to understand would be mocked as a fool.

Anyone, that is, except Jesus.

Psalm 33:13-15 says, "The LORD looks down from heaven and sees the whole human race. From his throne he observes all who live on the earth. He made their hearts, so he understands everything they do."

That's the understanding Jesus brought with him when he came to earth. And people got glimpses of it even in his early years. Once, when he was only twelve, he was found in the temple discussing profound questions with the religious leaders. Luke 2:47 says, "All who heard him were amazed at his understanding and his answers."

Years later, as his ministry took him from village to village, Jesus was able to connect with dysfunctional, messed-up people whom the rest of society had long since kicked to the curb. And not just connect with them, but dramatically impact their lives for the better. Part of the reason was because he understood them. Behavior patterns that seemed unfathomable to everyone else made perfect sense to the one who had made their hearts.

A striking example is his encounter with a Samaritan woman at Jacob's well.

THE WONDER AT THE WELL

She came to the well alone, which was a subtle but clear indication that she had few, if any, friends. In those days, fetching water was women's work, and they happily turned the task into a social event. Their evening walks to the well (which was about a half mile from the village) gave them a welcome break from household chores and a cherished opportunity to catch up on the latest gossip. The only reason a woman would go to the well alone in the scorching midday heat was if she didn't fit in or wasn't welcome with the rest of the girls.

And it's easy to understand why this woman wouldn't have fit in. Somewhere along the line, her life had veered terribly off course. A poor choice here, a wrong turn there, and suddenly her little-girl dreams of a fairy-tale life were gone. Forever, she must have assumed. With a long string of failed marriages on her résumé, not to mention the current live-in boyfriend, she was the woman everyone whispered about. And avoided.

She couldn't have known when she arrived at the well that she was keeping a divine appointment. Her intent was to fill her pitcher and head home. Get out of the hot sun as quickly as possible. Oh, how she would have belly-laughed at the notion that she, the town floozy, was about to have a life-changing experience that would be talked about till the end of time. And a *spiritual* experience to boot. But that's exactly what happened—because Almighty God was sitting by the well, just waiting for her arrival.

Oh, he didn't look like Almighty God. Not sitting there wiping sweat off his forehead and wheezing raspy words out of a parched throat. But God he was, in the flesh, eager to share words of kindness and love with a woman who had all but forgotten what they sounded like.

Volumes have been written about the things Jesus said to this woman. In particular, his comments about worshiping in spirit and truth are considered foundational. But to fully appreciate Jesus' compassionate understanding, we must give some thought to what he *didn't* say. He didn't enumerate her sins, lecture her for setting a bad example, ask for an explanation, demand an apology, or tell her she was going to Hell if she didn't shape up. It's hard to imagine a minister standing face-to-face with the biggest sinner in town—a woman whose life would have made a great *Jerry Springer* episode—and not even broaching the subject of morality, but that's what Jesus did.

Why?

Because he understood that she'd been hammered enough. Nobody knew better than she did what a mess she'd made of her life. She lived with the consequences of her choices every day and slept with them every night. What she needed was not another rebuke, but a deep, refreshing drink of living water.

I love John 4:28. It says that after talking with Jesus, the woman "left her water jar beside the well" and headed back toward town. Have you ever had an unexpected encounter so world-shaking that it caused you to forget what you were doing? I can picture Jesus noticing the forgotten water jar and smiling at the symbolism. She'd not only brought an empty jar to the well, she'd brought an empty life. And she was leaving both behind.

I also love the stir this woman created when she got back into town. Keep in mind, she wouldn't have been a popular figure. People would have distanced themselves from her. But on this day her message was so intriguing and her enthusiasm so contagious that even her harshest critics were filled with curiosity. "Come and meet a man who told me everything I ever did!" she said (John 4:29).

And they did. Followed her out to the well as if she were the Pied Piper of Hamelin.

Such is the power of a changed life.

One day in a sermon, I asked my people to imagine putting together a spiritual résumé. I urged them to think about what they would be able to include in terms of ministry experience and number of people led to the Lord. After the service, a man walked up to me and said, "Mark, I don't have a résumé. I have a rap sheet." We both laughed, but I knew he was only half joking.

Spiritually speaking, do you have more of a rap sheet than a résumé? Do you, like the woman at the well, have a long list of failures on your record? And do you find little reason to hope that your rap sheet won't continue to grow? Maybe you're in the middle of yet another spiritual crisis even as you read this book. Perhaps the same old sin that has caused you so much misery in the past has you in its grip again and has drained the faith right out of you.

If so, let me remind you of some important truths that should enable you to breathe a huge sigh of relief.

JESUS UNDERSTANDS YOUR PROBLEM

When I was a boy, my best friend and I had a whole sack full of little green army men. They were about an inch and a half tall, made of plastic, and formed into various postures and positions: running, tossing grenades, aiming rifles, and so on. We used to play with them in my friend's backyard where the grass was sparse and there was plenty of loose dirt. By using our hands and a small spade, we were able to shape the dirt and make our own little battlefield, complete with roads, bunkers, and elaborate forts. We even dug streams and rivers, used the garden hose to fill them with water, and built bridges over them with wooden rulers and Popsicle sticks. Some of our layouts were pretty impressive.

But they never lasted.

No matter how much time we spent building our battlefield, it was always a wreck by the next morning. If the wind didn't blow it away and the rain didn't wash it away, my buddy's collie would stomp through it fifty times or decide to stretch out and take a nap on top of it. But this never upset us. In fact, we expected it. Even as ten-year-olds, we understood that things made out of dust are weak and fragile.

You may never have thought about it before, but you too are made out of dust. Genesis 2:7 says, "And the LORD God formed a man's body from the dust of the ground and breathed into it the breath of life." This is why you're so weak. Why you're never able to be as good as you want to be. Why you've ended up chucking every

New Year's resolution you've ever made—before Groundhog Day. And why the same old temptations keep tripping you up over and over again.

Many people are confused, alarmed, or worried about their inability to stay on the straight and narrow. Even the apostle Paul said, "I don't understand myself at all, for I really want to do what is right, but I don't do it. Instead, I do the very thing I hate" (Romans 7:15). But our weakness isn't a mystery. We're weak because we're human. This is easily the biggest problem we face when it comes to trying to live godly lives.

The good news is that our Lord understands our problem and takes it into consideration in his dealings with us. Psalm 103:13, 14 says, "The LORD is like a father to his children, tender and compassionate to those who fear him. For he understands how weak we are; he knows we are only dust."

Several years ago a man I know was going through the painful process of trying to break an addiction. One day he asked me if I would jot down a list of encouraging Scriptures that he could carry with him at all times. Happy to do it, I chose ten of my favorites, typed them up, and handed the list to him at church. A few weeks later, I asked him if he still had the list and was using it. He said he was, and that the Scripture he found most encouraging was number six on the list, none other than Psalm 103:13, 14.

He said he'd grown up with the notion that Jesus was a strict disciplinarian who was watching his every move, just waiting for him to slip up. He said the guilt and fear that image created in him was paralyzing. Then he read David's words from Psalm 103, and it was as if the sun broke through the clouds. The words "tender" and "compassionate" were words he'd never associated with God. Suddenly, he had a whole new appreciation for Jesus, a deeper love for him than ever before, and a stronger desire than ever to try to please him.

Right now, if you're struggling with sin, don't give up. Keep fighting the good fight. And don't beat yourself up if you stumble. Jesus certainly wouldn't. He understands your problem.

But that's not all. . . .

Jesus Understands Your Position

Usually, when I see kids throwing tantrums in stores, I feel for the parents. But recently I witnessed a preschooler's meltdown and felt sorry for the kid. His mother was walking him through the toy department. She'd obviously told him she wasn't buying him anything, which I have no problem with. But she took it an unreasonable step further and told the little guy that he couldn't even *touch* anything. I happened to be standing beside them when he reached out for a Spider-Man motorcycle. His mother slapped his little hand away and said, "Don't touch!" The boy, who was already whining, burst into tears and started stomping his feet, which brought an unnecessarily harsh scolding from his mother.

As I walked away shaking my head, I had two thoughts. The first was that it's really hard for a three-year-old to be surrounded by toys that he's not allowed to touch. The second was that it's equally hard for adults.

We live in a world that is filled with tantalizing temptations. I was reminded of this recently when I walked outside to retrieve our mail. There, nestled in among the sale flyers and credit card offers, was the Victoria's Secret Christmas catalog. When I walked back into the house, I held it up to Marilyn and said, "Ho, ho, ho! 'Tis the season to be jolly!" which drew a reaction from her that was not unlike the one the preschooler got when he tried to touch the Spider-Man motorcycle.

We live in a titillating, tantalizing world that is not our home (Hebrews 13:14). A world where there will always be temptations to sin (Luke 17:1). A world where even an innocent trip to the mailbox can raise both your eyebrows and your blood pressure. Yet we've been instructed not to look at (Proverbs 4:25-27), touch (2 Corinthians 6:17), or even think about such things (Philippians 4:8).

That is one difficult position to be in.

But we can take heart because Jesus understands.

Hebrews 4:15 says that Jesus "understands our weaknesses, for he faced all of the same temptations we do, yet he did not sin."

I know it probably gives you the heebie-jeebies to think about Jesus looking at a pretty girl and having a sensual thought pass through his mind. But according to Scripture, he did. Surely, this at least partly explains why he showed such grace to the woman caught in adultery (John 8:1-11). As the Jewish leaders dragged the disheveled woman into his presence and threw her at his feet, he might well have been thinking back to a moment when he had experienced temptation.

But it's not just sexual sin. He must also have been tempted to lie, curse, cheat, steal, and punch somebody's lights out. Again, Hebrews says he faced "all of the same temptations we do." Not *some* of the same temptations. Not a *few* of the same temptations. But *all* of the same temptations.

This is a second reason why you should be able to breathe a huge sigh of relief. Not only does Jesus understand your problem, he understands your position.

And there's one more thing. . . .

Jesus Understands Your Pain

Once, when my parents were visiting from Illinois, I needed to run to the hospital to see one of our church members who'd had open-heart surgery the day before. My dad, who's had a multiple-bypass operation himself, asked if he could tag along. He said, "Don't worry. I'll stay out of the way."

But when we got to the patient's room, a powerful dynamic took over. When I told the man we were visiting that my dad had had the same surgery, he lost all interest in me. He turned his attention to my dad and started asking questions. The next thing

I knew, Dad had pulled a chair up beside the bed and the two of them were sharing experiences I couldn't begin to relate to. I had to smile as I stood back and watched the two of them bond. I knew I was observing the awesome power of shared suffering.

It's the same power that helped Jesus and the Samaritan woman make a heart-level connection in spite of their vast differences. As she approached the well, Jesus didn't just see a woman with a problem or a woman in a tough position. He also saw a woman in deep pain. A woman who'd had her heart broken at least five times. It was the kind of pain he could relate to.

Jesus wasn't married and never suffered the indignity of a divorce, but don't think for a moment that he didn't know what it feels like to get dumped. Isaiah 53:3 says, "He was despised and rejected." And indeed he was. He saw the people of his hometown reject him (Mark 6:3). He watched many of his followers lose interest and walk away (John 6:66). And he felt the sting of abandonment from his closest friends in his greatest hour of need (Mark 14:50).

Isaiah 53:3 also says that Jesus was "a man of sorrows, acquainted with bitterest grief." One evening the members of my small group were discussing that verse, and someone asked an intriguing question: what, exactly, *is* the "bitterest" grief? Is there one pain that outweighs all others? One hurt that has no equal? We threw out all sorts of possibilities: divorce, the death of a mate, the death of a child, Alzheimer's, cancer . . . But in the end we decided that the "bitterest" grief is the one you happen to be going through at the moment.

That's the perfect answer.

And the perfect message for hurting believers everywhere.

Whatever agony you happen to be going through right now, Jesus is acquainted with it. Don't be fooled by the fact that he lived a couple thousand years ago. Satan would love for you to think that because Jesus didn't live during our hectic, complicated times, he couldn't possibly understand what you're going through. Not true. Pain is pain, whether you're wearing a tunic and sandals or Dockers and a Polo. And Jesus had plenty of pain. More than enough to understand how you feel.

Perhaps the most shocking word in the Bible is found in Isaiah 53:10: "The LORD was pleased to crush Him, putting Him to grief" (*NASB*).

Do you see?

It's the fourth word in.

The word "pleased."

God was pleased to crush Jesus and put him to grief.

That's some serious double-take material, don't you agree? Why would any father, much less a loving father, be pleased to crush his son? If you're a parent, can you conceive of any circumstance that would make you pleased to crush one of your children?

But it's true. God was pleased to crush Jesus, and there's a very important reason why. He knew that crushing Jesus was the only way to build a bridge of understanding between Heaven and earth. Without that bridge, we would feel cut off and alone in times of temptation and suffering. We would feel that God didn't understand or, worse, that he didn't care. But because Jesus was also crushed, all such thoughts are banished.

Right now, you can rest assured that Jesus understands.

Your problem.

Your position.

And your pain.

topping it off

1. *Many of our most frustrating moments come when we desperately need understanding and can't seem to find it.* Outline the details of a time when you were misunderstood. How did being misunderstood make you feel? What did you do to try to correct the problem? Why do you think we are so desperate to be understood?

2. *There are unfathomable human mysteries all around us.* Do you have a tendency to try to analyze or explain other people's bad behavior? Why is it pointless to do this?

3. *It's hard to imagine a minister standing face-to-face with the biggest sinner in town—a woman whose life would have made a great Jerry Springer episode—and not even broaching the subject of morality, but that's what Jesus did.* What can we learn from Jesus' encounter with

the woman at the well about how to approach people with tangled lives who consistently make bad choices?

4. *I know it probably gives you the heebie-jeebies to think about Jesus looking at a pretty girl and having a sensual thought pass through his mind. But according to Scripture, he did.* Does it make you uncomfortable to think about Jesus having all the same impulses and desires that you have? Why is it important that we embrace this truth?

5. *Whatever agony you happen to be going through right now, Jesus is acquainted with it.* Think about the pain in your heart at this moment. What do you know about Jesus that helps you believe he understands how you feel?

REFILLING YOUR FAITH IN HIS PRESENCE

MATTHEW 14:22-33

I believe in the sun even if it isn't shining. I believe in love even when I am alone. I believe in God, even when He is silent.

—UNKNOWN

The Web site made a bold promise:

Jesus is all around you. Click *here* to see him!

I admit it. I moved my cursor over the link and left-clicked. Instantly, one of those inkblot optical illusions appeared on my screen. Underneath it were instructions to stare at the blot for thirty seconds and then look at a blank wall. I did, and sure enough, the image of a man's face appeared. But was it Jesus? I wasn't sure. It seemed to me that the image bore a striking resemblance to Charles Manson.

After Jesus (or Charles) faded into oblivion, I looked back at my computer screen and scrolled down. At the bottom of the page I found this suggestion:

"If you want to be reminded that Jesus is with you wherever you go, print this illusion and carry it with you in your pocket or your purse. When trouble comes, simply pull it out, stare at it for a few seconds, and you will see him all around you!"

But that's not the only weird thing I ran across as I was researching this chapter. Equally odd was the story of an Ohio woman who was grilling a pierogi on Easter Sunday.[1] When she flipped it over in the skillet, she was stunned to see Jesus' face flawlessly burned into the bread. At least, she assumed it was Jesus' face. After all, it *was* Easter Sunday, and the face had the obligatory long hair and beard. Was Jesus trying to tell her something? Was he really right there in the skillet, staring up through the slots in her spatula? As these and other profound spiritual questions raced through her mind, a far greater thought exploded like a nuclear warhead and obliterated them all:

Ebay!

With the tender care of a brain surgeon, the woman slipped the pierogi into a plastic bag and placed it in her freezer for safekeeping. From a purely financial standpoint, it was a savvy move. The online auction drew over 50,000 hits and a final sale price of $1,775.

As I read these and other equally off-the-wall stories, a famous quote from Albert Einstein came to mind. He said, "Only two things are infinite: the universe and human stupidity. And I'm not sure about the universe."[2] But then another, more gracious possibility occurred to me. Maybe the people who carry Jesus inkblots in their wallets and bid on Jesus pierogies aren't so much stupid as desperate. Maybe at least some of them are sincerely—desperately—trying to find a way to experience Jesus' presence and just don't know what else to do.

One thing is certain: feeling that the Lord is out of touch or out of reach is one of the most terrifying experiences a believer can have. David described the desperation well: "My God, my God! Why have you forsaken me? Why do you remain so distant? Why do you ignore my cries for help? Every day I call to you, my God, but you do not answer. Every night you hear my voice, but I find no relief. . . . You have laid me in the dust and left me for dead" (Psalm 22:1, 2, 15).

Can you relate? If your faith needs a refill, I'm guessing you can. In fact, this may be the primary reason *why* your faith has run dry. Maybe you, like David, have been crying out to God but getting no answers. Perhaps you're going through a crisis at this very moment and have prayed yourself hoarse, but nothing has happened. Or maybe things have gotten worse since you started praying, leaving you to stare up at the vast, starlit heavens and plead, "My God, my God! Why have you forsaken me?" And maybe—*just maybe*—if someone offered you a Jesus inkblot or a Jesus pierogi right about now, you'd figure you had nothing to lose by taking it.

The good news is that God knew we would experience such feelings, and he placed several powerful stories in the Bible to help us overcome them. One of my favorites is found in Matthew 14.

TAUGHT BY A TEMPEST

David Copperfield became an international celebrity by performing illusions that pale in comparison to what Jesus did for real one evening on a remote hillside near Nazareth. He took five loaves of bread and two fish and biggie-sized them into a feast for more than five thousand hungry people. You wouldn't think there could possibly be a downside to such a wonderful miracle, but there was. The people became starstruck and immediately started a grassroots campaign to make Jesus their king (John 6:15). This, of course, was the last thing he wanted. The second-to-last thing he wanted was for his disciples to get caught up in such a ridiculous movement, so he hustled them into a boat and sent them to the other side of the Sea of Galilee. Then he went off to a quiet spot to pray and unwind.

At some point after the disciples set sail, a real-life *Gilligan's Island* scenario began to unfold. The weather started getting rough. The tiny ship was tossed. If not for the courage of the fearless crew . . . well, you get the idea. The Sea of Galilee, sometimes called the Lake of Gennesaret, was seven miles wide, fifteen miles long, and well known as a nasty place to be during a storm. A valley to the north acted as a natural wind tunnel, creating violent squalls with waves that often exceeded ten feet. Under such conditions, even the most experienced seamen would be taxed to the limits of their expertise just to keep their boat from capsizing.

The Bible says the disciples set sail before nightfall (Matthew 14:22, 23) and were still locked in mortal combat with the storm at three o'clock in the morning (v. 25)! Imagine the muscle fatigue and cramps they must have been experiencing as they hoisted the heavy oars for up to nine hours. Calluses would have ripped open and bled. And the elements would only have added to their agony. If you've ever been caught outside in a violent storm, you know that a driving wind can make raindrops feel like pin pricks. And a heavy wave crashing across your back might just as well be a two-by-four.

It's easy to believe the disciples were nearing the end of their physical and emotional endurance when Jesus approached them, walking on the water. It's easier still to understand why they thought he was a ghost. At that time, the seas were thought to be full of evil spirits. And any director of B-grade horror movies will tell you that few visuals are more terrifying than the fleeting glimpse of an unidentified figure in a flash of lightning. Put it all together and you have pure Hitchcock. It was likely the scariest moment the disciples had ever known.

Understanding this, Jesus spoke: "It's all right. I am here! Don't be afraid" (Matthew 14:27).

Often, Bible students slide right over these words because they're so anxious to get to the next section of the story, which tells about Peter walking on the water. Not being natural water walkers, we are endlessly fascinated by the idea. I'm guessing that more sermons have been preached about Peter's wave walk than any other non-Christmas or non-Easter story in the Gospels. In fact, the saying "You can't walk on water if you don't get out of the boat" has become a cliché in our culture.

But any person who feels abandoned by the Lord needs to slam on the brakes at verse 27. The nine words Jesus spoke in the midst of that terrible storm are some of the most important ever to come out of his mouth. They are both comforting and challenging.

The Comfort

Picture an airliner, loaded with passengers, flying through a storm. Severe turbulence is jostling people in their seats and scaring them worse than a Bob Dylan vocal solo. Children are crying, adults are repenting, and people of all ages are pulling out their little white paper bags—and using them! Then, suddenly, a flight attendant steps into the aisle holding her trusty microphone. With a reassuring smile, she says, "It's all right. I am here. Don't be afraid."

How do you think her words would be received?

Or imagine that your closest loved one is undergoing a life-threatening surgery. The doctors have warned you that his chances of survival are only about fifty-fifty. The surgery was supposed to last four hours, but now five have passed and the surgeon's still not finished. Fear is pressing so hard against your solar plexus that you can barely breathe. But then your Uncle Joe, an auto mechanic from Toledo, walks into the waiting room, smiles, and says, "It's all right. I am here. Don't be afraid."

Would your fear suddenly evaporate?

You see my point, don't you?

Whether or not these nine words are comforting depends on whose mouth they come out of. If the person saying them has no power over the circumstances at hand, the words end up sounding like a pathetic joke. Thankfully, our Lord has proven himself well qualified to speak these words by demonstrating his power over the two greatest causes of human misery: the elements and the enemy.

Jesus controls the elements

We Floridians have seen six major hurricanes slam into our state in the last year. Whenever a nasty one bubbles up in the tropics, all the highfalutin weather experts take to the airwaves . . . but not to actually *do* anything about the storm. They've got enough high-tech instruments to make the weather station look like NASA Mission Control, but they can't make the storm fizzle out or change its course. The very best they can hope for is to predict the track it will take. And sometimes even *that* proves impossible.

But such things are child's play for our Lord.

He can create a storm when he wants to (Jonah 1:4), turn one on a dime (Job 37:15), or stop one in an instant (Luke 8:24). Best of all, he can protect his people when they're in the middle of one (Isaiah 32:2).

But it's not just storms.

Our Lord controls every aspect of nature. Job 9:7 says, "If he commands it, the sun won't rise and the stars won't shine." Nor will the wind blow, the rain fall, the fire burn, or the earth quake. He's proven that he can part seas (Exodus 14:21), cause water to gush out of a rock (Exodus 17:6), make the sun stand still (Joshua 10:13), and keep fire from burning (Daniel 3:25). Our Lord controls the elements.

Jesus controls the enemy

I love the story about the demon-possessed man Jesus met when he arrived in the land of the Gerasenes (Mark 5:1-20). The poor, tormented soul must have looked like he just stepped off the set of the *Texas Chainsaw Massacre*. He lived among the tombs and howled like an animal. He practiced self-mutilation. And he could not be contained. In their fear, the townspeople sent their strongest men to try to capture him, but their chains might just as well have been made of paper for all the good they did.

The Bible says that the evil spirits that were torturing the man had a "spokesdemon" who saw Jesus approaching and began pleading with him not to torture them (v. 7). Interesting, don't you think? The confrontation hadn't even started yet, and the demons were already acknowledging defeat and negotiating terms of surrender!

And what about the fact that Jesus was outnumbered? He was one Lord against many demons (v. 9), but they were still helpless to resist his commands.

This is why the apostle Paul, when writing about the enemy's attacks against us, said, "Be strong with the Lord's mighty power" (Ephesians 6:10). He knew that we'd never be able to defeat Satan through our own power. We'd never be able to outrun, outfox, or outmaneuver him. Our only hope is to lean on the only one who *can* control him.

Some of the storms we face will be element driven, like when a tornado is bearing down on your house or a tumor shows up on your CAT scan. Others will be enemy driven, like when a flirty little, size 4 secretary decides she likes *your* husband better than her own. Either way, you can take comfort. The one who controls both the elements *and* the enemy is saying, "It's all right. I am here! Don't be afraid."

The Challenge

But there's more than comfort in these words. There's also a challenge. Jesus doesn't say "Try not to be afraid." He says, "*Don't be afraid.*" He lays it down as a command, knowing full well that our tendency toward fear is our greatest weakness.

If you doubt this, consider that we are born with only two fears: the fear of falling and the fear of loud noises. But by the time we reach adulthood, our fears have become so numerous and so exotic that the word *fear* just doesn't seem to do them justice anymore. So we call them phobias. And we slap prefixes on them so we can tell them apart. As of this writing, there are 524 phobias that have been identified.[3] My favorite is *hippopotomonstrosesquippedaliophobia*, which is the fear of long words.

When Jesus says "Don't be afraid," he's meeting us at the point of our biggest weakness. He's challenging us to do something that goes completely against our nature. And he often forces us to wrestle with that challenge for a while by temporarily withholding his power. When he walked on the water toward the disciples, he spoke words of comfort to them and challenged them to let go of their fears. But he didn't immediately calm the storm. He allowed it to go right on raging!

When I was in elementary school, I sat beside a rather strange kid who amused himself by catching flies and playing with them. Naturally, he had to disable their flying apparatus, which seems more gruesome now than it did then. But the flies, other than being permanently grounded, didn't seem to show any ill effects. I still remember the time he drew a starting line and a finish line on a piece of notebook paper and had races with two of his captives while the teacher was waxing eloquent about history or math or something else slightly more important—but not nearly as entertaining to a couple of fourth-grade boys.

Have you ever felt as though God was that strange kid and you were the fly? Have you ever thought that he must be toying with you . . . that he must be enjoying watching you suffer and struggle? I hate to say it, but I have. There have been times of prolonged difficulty in my life when I've looked heavenward and said, "Excuse me, Lord, but in case you haven't noticed, I could use a little help here!" But even then, nothing happened.

Do you ever wonder why he does that?

I've come to understand that when God doesn't calm our storms as quickly as we'd like, it's because he's trying to teach us something. Specifically, he's trying to teach us the very thing he's *always* trying to teach us: who he really is.

Oh sure, the Bible *tells* us who he is. He's our fortress (Psalm 18:2), our hiding place (Psalm 32:7), our portion (Psalm 119:57, *NASB*), our Father (Psalm 89:26), and our deliverer (Psalm 70:5, *NIV*) . . . among other things. But how do we really know for sure until we experience these attributes in real-life situations? Author Ron Mehl says it beautifully:

How do I know He's my Fortress until, with arrows flying all around me, I run with all my heart into His open gates?

How do I know He's my Hiding Place until I hear the enemy crashing in the brush behind me, feel his breath on the back of my neck, and cry out for a place of refuge?

How do I know He's my Portion until all I treasure and hold dear is suddenly threatened or taken from me?

How do I know He's my Father until I feel orphaned and abandoned and left alone in the storm?

How do I—like Peter—learn that He's my Deliverer until I step out of the boat and plant my foot on fifty fathoms of frothy sea?[4]

It's one thing to be told something is true. It's another thing to be *shown*. God has established his Word to tell us who he is, but he still uses circumstances to show us. That's why you shouldn't despair when you find yourself in a storm that doesn't seem to be letting up. It doesn't mean you've been abandoned. It doesn't mean God has suffered a power failure or that he enjoys watching you suffer. It simply means there's some aspect of his character that he wants you to discover—or at least appreciate more than you have in the past.

If Jesus had immediately calmed the storm that had the disciples stretched to the limit of their endurance, they would have been grateful, and they would have known that Jesus could calm a storm. But by allowing the storm to rage a little longer and by enabling Peter to take a stroll on the waves, Jesus was demonstrating more than what he could do *to* a storm. He was demonstrating what he could do *in* a storm. For Peter and the rest of the disciples, who would one day be enduring storms of persecution as they led the early church, this was a critical lesson.

Psalm 46:1 says, "God is our refuge and strength, an ever-present help in trouble" (*NIV*). There's little doubt Peter knew this verse. But after his storm experience on the Sea of Galilee, he could honestly say he'd *lived* it. And living it beats knowing it every time.

A Word of Caution

A common error made by many believers is that they assume the Lord's presence is always going to be indicated by some sort of dramatic event.

Not long ago a member of our church attended another congregation with a friend. At that service, there was a period of unrestrained tongues-speaking that morphed into a prolonged free-for-all of hysterical laughter. For almost fifteen minutes, the entire congregation roared like a group of adolescent boys at a *Napoleon Dynamite* showing. According to my friend, some people even ended up lying on the floor and flopping like fish. When order was finally restored, the pastor referred to the spectacle as "proof positive" that the Spirit of the Lord was in the room. Naturally, the people screamed, whistled, and applauded their approval of his statement.

I'm sorry, but I'm not buying it.

Nowhere does the Bible teach that the Lord's presence is always going to be indicated by some dramatic event. In fact, God makes the very opposite point in 1 Kings 19. In that chapter, he planted a discouraged Elijah on a mountain, where he witnessed a wind so mighty that it actually started breaking the mountain apart! Then he saw an earthquake, and after that, a fire. But the Bible specifically says that God was not in the wind, the earthquake, or the fire. They were *not* indicators of his presence.

What *was?* A "gentle whisper" (v. 12).

Mark it down. Sometimes our Lord's presence is so dramatic it's unmistakable, such as in the storm account we just explored. But at other times it's so subtle it's easy to miss. Isn't that one of the great lessons we learn from the Christmas story? Almighty God's arrival in Bethlehem was so quiet and unassuming that people just a few feet away didn't even notice!

I'm convinced that God's "gentle whispers" often get drowned out by all the hubbub of our boisterous lives. Why else would he command us to "be silent" and know that he is God (Psalm 46:10)? And why else would David say that he waits "quietly" before God (Psalm 62:5)? I also believe that those who teach that God's presence is always indicated by dramatic events will be forced to manufacture them on those days when he chooses to whisper.

So rejoice in the Lord's presence. Find comfort in his promise to be with you always (Matthew 28:20). But don't expect him to always rock your world. It should be enough just to know he is near.

topping it off

1. *One thing is certain: feeling that the Lord is out of touch or out of reach is one of the most terrifying experiences a believer can have.* Have you ever felt that God was out of your reach? What happened to make you feel that way? What did you do to try to overcome that feeling? Did it work?

2. *Jesus doesn't say "Try not to be afraid." He says, "Don't be afraid." He lays it down as a command, knowing full well that our tendency toward fear is our greatest weakness.* Are there times when you feel that our Lord's commands are unreasonable? Why do you think he sets the bar so high, when he knows how weak we are?

3. *It's one thing to be told something is true. It's another thing to be shown. God has established his Word to tell us who he is, but he still uses circumstances to show us.* Can you think of a time when God used circumstances to teach you a great truth? What happened? How has your life changed because of that lesson?

4. *I'm convinced that God's "gentle whispers" often get drowned out by all the hubbub of our boisterous lives.* How long has it been since you spent some quiet time alone with God simply to enjoy his presence? Do you have a regular quiet time? What specific steps can you take to lower the decibel level of your life?

3
REFILLING YOUR FAITH IN HIS WORDS

MATTHEW 8:23-27

All that the gospels report of what Jesus said, in private and in public, he could have uttered in two hours. . . . But think of it! To be able to say in two hours enough to change the current of mankind!

—EDGAR J. GOODSPEED

John Edward Robinson Sr. was as friendly a fellow as you'd ever want to meet.[1] Married for thirty-eight years, he was a good provider, helped raise four upstanding children, and was his grandkids' favorite babysitter. Because of his sunny disposition and civic involvement, friends and neighbors adored him and considered him an asset to the community.

But John Robinson had a dark secret.

While his wife was at work, he sat at his computer and prowled sexy Internet chat rooms. He presented himself to vulnerable women as the perfect man: mature, financially stable, and, of course, incurably romantic. He talked of his life accomplishments and unfulfilled dreams, never once mentioning that he was a married grandfather. Instead, he spoke of his longing for someone with whom to share his wonderful life.

To say that John Robinson had a way with words would be an understatement. Many women found him charming and irresistible. So charming and irresistible that a few even packed up their belongings and moved to the small Kansas town where he lived. These included Izabela Lewicka, a nineteen-year-old college student who was attending Purdue University. Though Robinson was over thirty years her senior, she was mesmerized by his e-mails and convinced that she'd never know another day of happiness if she didn't drop out of school and go live near him. Naturally, her parents and friends were alarmed and urged her not to do it, but her fierce determination caused them to back off and let her go. Secretly, they hoped the relationship would crash and burn and that she would be back home by the start of the next semester.

It was a false hope.

On June 3, 2000, law enforcement officials searched a farm Robinson owned near La Cygne, Kansas. They found Izabela's badly decomposed body stuffed inside an 85-gallon barrel. John Robinson turned out to be more than just a naughty man looking for kicks on the Net. Today he sits on death row and is recognized as the first serial killer to use the Internet as a stalking ground. He is known to have murdered at least eight women, all of whom he met online.

There are many lessons to be learned from a story like this, not the least of which is that words are extraordinarily powerful. When John Robinson and Izabela Lewicka had their initial contact online, there were no facial expressions. There was no voice inflection or body language. Their words were fired into cyberspace completely raw, without any audio or visual enhancements. Yet, his words contained such power that he still managed to completely captivate her.

Thankfully, word power can be used for good too.

In March 2005, Ashley Smith was living the saddest of lives.[2] Four years earlier, her husband had been stabbed in a fight and died in her arms. Since then, she had become a drug addict whose crystal meth habit had rotted her teeth, thinned her hair, and made her give up custody of her only child. Then, in what could only be described as a crash landing on rock bottom, she was taken hostage by Brian Nichols, an escaped convict who'd murdered four people earlier in the day. Not even the most cockeyed optimist would have given her a snowball's chance of surviving the ordeal.

But survive she did.

As Nichols held Ashley at gunpoint in her own apartment, she began reading to him from Rick Warren's mega best seller, *The Purpose Driven Life*. The words had a calming effect on both captor and captive, and triggered a lengthy conversation about life's purpose and meaning. That conversation—held over the barrel of a loaded gun—was clearly a turning point in the ordeal. Everyone believes the words Ashley read and spoke in that tiny apartment were the reason why Brian Nichols chose not only to spare her life but also to let her go unharmed.

It's impossible to overestimate the power of words. They can injure or heal, poison or nourish, deceive or enlighten, cost lives or save them. It is no exaggeration to say that the course of history can be changed with a single sentence.

In 1987, Ronald Reagan met with Russian Premier Gorbachev in Berlin. Everybody knows that certain protocols come into play when heads of state get together. Above all, you're supposed to act like friends, smile for the cameras, and not say anything in public that might embarrass your counterpart. But Reagan threw such conventional thinking right out the window and dared to speak six words that historians agree altered the world forever: "Mr. Gorbachev, tear down this wall!"

When I think about that incident, I'm reminded that James compared the tongue to a small bit that can turn a powerful horse, or a tiny rudder that can alter the direction of an enormous ship (James 3:3, 4).

In 1 Kings 10, the Queen of Sheba paid a visit to King Solomon. She'd heard that he was a pretty smart guy, so she wanted to test him with hard questions. Verse 3 says, "Solomon answered all her questions; nothing was too hard for the king to explain to her." The Bible says that his answers literally took her breath away (v. 5).

That's pretty impressive, but not as impressive as Jesus.

No words ever written or spoken can compare with those of our Lord. Those who were privileged to hear him said, "We have never heard anyone talk like this!" (John 7:46). What makes that statement especially powerful is that it didn't come from family or friends who might have been partial. It came from the temple guards who'd been sent to arrest him! They were so moved by his words that they couldn't bring themselves to lay a hand on him.

Remember when the Pharisees dragged a woman caught in adultery before our Lord? It's likely that they'd set her up to be caught; in any case they were delighted to have an opportunity to put Jesus in what appeared to be a hopeless situation. If he upheld the Jewish law and condoned her stoning, he would appear legalistic and unsympathetic. But if he ordered her to be set free, he would be accused of breaking the law. I suspect the Pharisees could barely contain their snickers.

Until Jesus did the unexpected.

Two times he knelt and wrote in the dust. What, we don't know. Likely, it wasn't more than a few words. But whatever they were, they were powerful enough to drain the courage right out of some of the most evil men history has ever known, causing them to drop their rocks and go home (John 8:1-11). Speaking as one who makes his living with words, I find that scene utterly stunning. Even the world's greatest wordsmiths would never be able to produce that kind of response completely off the cuff, using only their index fingers and some loose dirt.

Truly, no one ever spoke (or wrote in the dirt) like Jesus.

Perhaps you've lost sight of this.

If you've been running low on faith, maybe it's because you've been listening to the wrong people. With talk radio and television blaring 24/7, with a record number of magazines in print, with thousands of publishers spitting out scores of books a year, and with superstores like Borders, Barnes & Noble, and Amazon.com offering them to us at discounted prices, we live under a Niagara-like torrent of verbiage. But how many of those words are truly worthy of your time and attention? How many are going to impact your life in any meaningful way?

Not that many, I'm afraid.

But one thing is sure: our Lord's words are packed with power and, given the chance, will make a dramatic difference in your life. In case you've forgotten what our Lord's words are capable of, let me take you back to an intense moment early in his ministry.

Sleeping Through a Storm

In Matthew 8, we find the disciples back out on the Sea of Galilee in another storm. Only this time, Jesus was in the boat with them. The Bible says the storm was "terrible" and that waves were "breaking into the boat" (v. 24). The disciples were fighting the storm for all they were worth, but they weren't getting any help from Jesus because he was sound asleep.

Several years ago, there was a story on the news about a man who got up one morning, stretched real good, and then opened his bedroom door only to discover that the rest of his house had been blown away by a tornado. Another story, equally as bizarre, had to do with a man who was asleep in his recliner one afternoon when an out-of-control car came crashing through the wall of his house. According to the report, the man didn't move a muscle until the driver of the car crawled out of the wreck and shook him awake.

As crazy as these stories sound when you first hear them, there are legitimate reasons why someone might sleep that soundly. For example, a person could be hard of hearing or on powerful medication or stone-cold drunk. We know that none of those possibilities were applicable to Jesus. So how can we explain his ability to sleep through such a violent storm?

For one thing, he must have been exhausted. From sunup to sundown, he was relentlessly about his Father's business: walking, teaching, listening, answering, explaining, counseling, and healing. Finally, there was the sheer weight of pressure he would have been carrying as the Savior of the world. God's eternal plan hinged completely on Jesus' ability to remain faithful and stay the course, yet every day there were evil men dogging his steps, trying everything they could think of to trip him up. How could he *not* have been weary?

But there's an even better reason why he was able to rest peacefully in the midst of such chaos. He had complete confidence in his heavenly Father's loving care. He would have echoed David's words of Psalm 4:8: "I will lie down in peace and sleep, for you alone, O Lord, will keep me safe."

Of course, we have the advantage of historical perspective as we contemplate this scene. We can see that everything turned out OK. But if we'd been in that boat fighting for our lives—bailing water, wrestling with the oars, and fighting a wayward sail—we would have been screaming at Jesus too. We wouldn't have given a rip about his fatigue, and we wouldn't have wanted to hear him quote any psalms. We would just have wanted him to wake up and do something!

Finally, he did.

He raised his head from the cushion and said, "Quiet down!" (Mark 4:39).

I've always wondered if the disciples thought he was talking to them. One thing we know for sure: the wind and the waves weren't confused. Instantly they obeyed. The bulging sail fell slack as the tilting vessel righted itself. The sea grew eerily calm as the disciples, soaking wet and on the verge of collapsing, looked at each other, wide-eyed. It was easily the most amazing thing they'd seen Jesus do up to that point. And he did it, not with a wave of his hand or a Samantha Stevens-like twitch of his nose, but with a few power-packed words.

If you've forgotten how powerful our Lord's words are, let this story refill your faith. His words still do now what they did then.

They Calm Storms

If you've ever been caught in a powerful storm, you know that chaos reigns. As hurricane Jeanne passed over our house in 2004, I looked out the window and saw two small oak trees in our backyard bending *toward* each other! The trees are not more than twenty feet apart, but the powerful winds were swirling in such a tight vortex that, at the same moment, one tree was leaning severely toward the north and the other was leaning severely toward the south.

During the same storm, my wife, Marilyn, and I kept hearing debris hitting the outside of our house. At one point, I heard something big and heavy slam against the wall just outside my office window. When I opened the blinds and looked out, I saw a long section of guttering flying across the yard like it was made out of Styrofoam. We never did find out who that gutter belonged to. It must have come from a block or more away.

Swirling winds and flying debris.

Chaos.

This is what storms produce. Not just the ones that form in the sky, but also the ones that form in our lives.

I was reminded of this just yesterday when I spoke with a young woman whose marriage is in deep trouble because of her husband's infidelity. Her swirling emotions have her leaning first one way and then another. One day she wants to fight for her husband, and the next she wants to strangle him. And talk about flying debris! The verbal hand grenades they're lobbing at each other are throwing shrapnel and leaving wounds that will likely take years to heal.

Can you relate? Are you caught in a storm of your own right now? Do you find that shifting emotional winds have you leaning first one way and then another? Have you been coldcocked by flying debris? Have things become so confusing that you don't even know what's right anymore? And are you so weary of it all that you almost don't even care? If so, remember that our Lord's words can bring order out of chaos.

This is one of the first truths the Bible teaches us.

In Genesis 1:2 we're told that the earth as God originally created it was "empty, a formless mass cloaked in darkness." Note the word "formless." It means "without structure or design." Or, in a word, chaotic. But then God began to speak—"Let there be light" (v. 3)—and suddenly that formless, chaotic mass began to take shape and get organized.

So it's no surprise to see Jesus speaking words that would calm a storm. He was just doing what he's done since the beginning of time. Using words to settle things down and bring order out of chaos has always been his specialty.

Maybe it's time you rediscovered this truth.

If your cup is running low on faith, you probably don't give as much attention to his words as you once did. Perhaps you can't even remember the last time you picked up your Bible, headed for a quiet spot, and started reading in earnest. But if there's a storm raging in your life, you desperately need to reconnect with the Scriptures. 2 Timothy 3:16 says that our Lord's Word "straightens us out." Isn't that exactly what you need when your life becomes hopelessly tangled and chaotic?

The calm you're craving is as close as your Bible. Somewhere within that book are the perfect words for your situation—words that may not change the circumstances you're facing but will calm the storm in your heart. Granted, you may have to work to find them. The Bible is a big book that addresses a lot of subjects. But with the help of a godly friend and a good reference book or two, you should have no problem.

Right now, before the storm batters you another day, I urge you to cast your lot with the psalmist, who said, "I am counting on the LORD; yes, I am counting on him. I have put my hope in his word" (Psalm 130:5).

His words calm storms.

But that's not all. . . .

They Answer Questions

We often don't ask the question that's really on our minds. Instead, we ask a different question—often a softer question—and hope the person we're speaking to is able to read between the lines and give us the information we really want.

For example, when a man's wife is giving him the cold shoulder for no apparent reason, he doesn't dare ask her why she's being rude and unkind. (Not unless he wants to spend the night on the couch.) Instead, he asks, "Are you feeling OK?"

And when a wife does a pirouette in front of her husband and asks him if he thinks her new dress looks good, that's not really what she wants to know. What she really wants to know is if he thinks *she* looks good.

Hidden messages and questions are embedded in much of the interaction that happens between people, and this incident with Jesus and the disciples is no exception. In Matthew's version, when the storm-weary disciples woke Jesus, they said, "Lord, save us! We're going to drown!" (Matthew 8:25). What they really meant is expressed better in Mark's version: "Teacher, don't you even care that we are going to drown?" (Mark 4:38).

Don't you even care?

This is the question that always burns in our hearts when trouble comes and our Lord doesn't seem to be doing anything to help us. It's a question produced by a faith running on fumes—a question we often hate ourselves for asking but can't seem to avoid. It's the question that was burning a hole in Job's heart when he said, "I cry to you, O God, but you don't answer me" (Job 30:20). And it's the question that tore a bitter wail from the psalmist: "I am forgotten, cut off from your care" (Psalm 88:5).

If your faith needs a refill, *Don't you even care?* may be the question you've been asking lately.

If so, you'll find your answer in the same place the disciples found theirs—in Jesus' words. When he said, "Quiet down!" he was commanding the storm, but even more so, he was sending a message to the disciples. He was saying, "See, I *do* care."

This is one of the most important things you can understand about Jesus' words. It doesn't matter who (or what) he's speaking to in Scripture, he's also speaking to you and me. Every sentence has significance, and woven throughout his words and phrases are the answers to all of life's most important questions. If a passage doesn't seem relevant, it's only because it doesn't meet your need at that particular moment. The probability is that someday it will.

Of course, a skeptic would argue this point. He would say that our Lord's words are insufficient and incomplete because there are some questions he flatly refuses to answer, such as the specific time of his second coming (Matthew 24:36).

The answer to this objection is that the mystery of when our Lord is coming back, though fascinating, doesn't qualify as one of life's most important questions. Not knowing the time of our Lord's return in no way hinders a believer's ability to live a happy life in harmony with God. In fact, you could make the case that *knowing* the time *would* be a hindrance because it would tempt us to wait until the last minute to repent or make needed changes in our lives.

And so it is with all the other questions our Lord has chosen not to answer. They may be tantalizing and intriguing, but they are not essential to our success as Christians. Paul made this point very clear when he said to Timothy, "The Lord will give you understanding in all these things" (2 Timothy 2:7). The prior verses indicate that "all these things" were the fundamental issues relating to the practical, daily execution of the Christian life. Essentially, he was saying that God has not left us to grope in the dark, to stagger and stumble toward eternity in a state of confusion.

His words calm storms and answer questions.

Finally . . .

They Create Fear

I know this doesn't sound like a good thing. Except for the people who spend their hard-earned money to see R-rated slasher films, nobody likes fear. But truth isn't always obvious, and this is a perfect example. You may never have thought about it before, but the fear of God is a critical component of the successful Christian life. I've never known a strong Christian who didn't have it, and I've never known a weak Christian who did.

Yes, yes, I know . . . the Bible tells us to "fear not." In fact, I recently heard a speaker claim that we're told not to be afraid 366 times in Scripture. "That's one 'fear not' for each day of the year, plus one," she said. I don't know if that's true, but I do know the Bible says it many times. However, not once does the Bible ever tell us not to be afraid of God. On the contrary, the fear of God is repeatedly exalted in Scripture. Read the following verses carefully:

- "Fear of the LORD is the beginning of wisdom" (Proverbs 9:10).
- "The LORD watches over those who fear him" (Psalm 33:18).
- "Sin whispers to the wicked, deep within their hearts. They have no fear of God to restrain them" (Psalm 36:1).
- "Dear friends, don't be afraid of those who want to kill you. They can only kill the body; they cannot do any more to you. But I'll tell you whom to fear. Fear God, who has the power to kill people and then throw them into hell" (Luke 12:4, 5).
- "The church then had peace throughout Judea, Galilee, and Samaria, and it grew in strength and numbers. The believers were walking in the fear of the Lord and in the comfort of the Holy Spirit" (Acts 9:31).

Clearly, God intends for us to fear him.

Now back to the disciples.

They were thrilled to have their storm calmed and to know that Jesus did indeed care about them. But Jesus calmed the storm in such a jaw-dropping way that they were completely stunned. Matthew records that they asked each other, "Who is this?" (8:27).

The significance of that question is found in a quirky little fact of life we seldom think about. It's simply that answers create more questions than they eliminate. Every discovery opens the door to new possibilities. The crest of every hill reveals new twists and turns in the road ahead.

Take the Wright Brothers, for example. Their primitive contraption lifted off the ground at Kitty Hawk, North Carolina, on December 17, 1903, and flew for a grand total of 120 feet in twelve seconds. During that twelve-second period, many questions were answered. But for every one that was answered, ten more were created. That's why, after a brief celebration, the brothers went scurrying back to their bicycle shop. They knew their research was just getting started.

Likewise, the disciples learned something important about Jesus when he calmed the wind and the waves. But that information opened the door to a thousand new possibilities, and some of them were truly frightening. They knew that someone who possessed that kind of power could do anything at any time. And he definitely would be the kind of person you wouldn't want to antagonize or disobey!

This is the value of godly fear.

From that day forward the disciples were, I'm confident, a little more attentive when Jesus spoke. I imagine they were a little quicker to obey when he made a request and a little slower to complain when he said something they didn't like.

If your faith reserves have been depleted, maybe you need the kind of jolt the disciples got that day on the Sea of Galilee. Maybe you need to be reminded of our Lord's awesome power and to think about the mind-boggling implications of it. To put it bluntly, maybe you've gotten a little cocky and need the fear of God put back in you.

Let me challenge you to get back into the Word, to rediscover what our Lord can do, and to let that knowledge frighten you . . . and set you free. The prophet Isaiah said, "Do not fear anything except the LORD Almighty. He alone is the Holy One. If you fear him, you need fear nothing else" (Isaiah 8:13).

Recently, Snickers has been running a bizarre commercial on television. It shows a man working in an office cubicle with Snickers candy bars taped to his bald head. He's wearing them as a toupee and looks perfectly ridiculous, but he's going about his business as if nothing in the world is wrong. This prompts three of his coworkers to approach his desk and say, "You can take the Snickers bars off of your head. They're not working. We *know* you're bald." The man then breaks down in tears, and the ad ends with the words, "It's only satisfying if you eat it."

Something similar could be said about God's Word.

It's only satisfying—it can only help you—if it's *in* you. That's what the apostle Peter was getting at when he said, "Like newborn babes, long for the pure milk of the word, that by it you may grow in respect to salvation" (1 Peter 2:2, *NASB*).

The Word.

Is it in *you?*

topping it off

1. *It's impossible to overestimate the power of words. They can injure or heal, poison or nourish, deceive or enlighten, cost lives or save them.* Have you ever been injured or healed by someone's words? Poisoned or nourished? Deceived or enlightened? What happened? How careful are you about the words you speak? Do you have a tendency to speak impulsively?

2. *We live under a Niagara-like torrent of verbiage. But how many of those words are truly worthy of your time and attention? How many are going to impact your life in any meaningful way?* What voices do you listen to the most? Have any of them ever given you bad advice? Is there a voice in your life right now that you would be better off tuning out? If so, how can you do this in a way that won't cause offense?

3. *Perhaps you can't even remember the last time you picked up your Bible, headed for a quiet spot, and started reading in earnest. But if there's a storm raging in your life, you desperately need to reconnect with the*

Scriptures. How often do you read your Bible? Do you feel this is enough? What's keeping you from spending even more time in the Word?

4. *And so it is with all the other questions our Lord has chosen not to answer. They may be tantalizing and intriguing, but they are not essential to our success as Christians.* What's a question you've always wondered about, but that God has chosen not to answer? Why do you think God feels the answer to this question is not important at the moment?

5. *"Do not fear anything except the Lord Almighty. He alone is the Holy One. If you fear him, you need fear nothing else" (Isaiah 8:13).* Describe what you think the fear of God should look like in a committed Christian's life. Is that how it looks in yours?

4
REFILLING YOUR FAITH IN HIS PROMISES

LUKE 5:1-11

All I have seen teaches me to trust the Creator for all I have not seen.

—RALPH WALDO EMERSON

I was in our local Publix supermarket, fourth in line at the pharmacy, waiting to pick up a prescription. Third in line was a young woman I wouldn't have traded places with for a million dollars. She was very attractive and seemed pleasant enough, but she had something in her shopping cart that struck fear in my heart: a three-year-old boy with an attitude.

The little guy had one thing on his mind, and that was to escape the prison that was his mother's cart. When he tried to climb out, she stopped him. He, in turn, produced wails of agony that I'm sure could be heard in the produce department at the other end of the store. "Please, Mommy!" he cried. "I want out!" But his mother was one tough cookie. She calmly explained to him that he could not get out of the cart because he would just run away, and she didn't feel like chasing him. Then she looked away and ignored him.

And he cranked up the volume.

Honestly, I don't think I've ever heard so much noise come out of such a little person. The kid was practically peeling the paint off the wall with his shrieks. And everybody was staring. In the end, I think that's what got to his mom. I had the feeling she was used to his tantrums, but she realized everyone else was suffering, so she finally took him by the shoulders and said, in her sternest voice, "If I let you out of this cart, do you promise to stay right here and not run away?" The little guy's head instantly started bobbing up and down. He was obviously willing to agree to any terms that would get his little feet on the floor. So his mom wiped his nose with a tissue she pulled out of her sleeve (why do mothers do that?) and lifted him out of the cart.

Conventional wisdom says that you should never negotiate with terrorists, and that day I was reminded of why. As soon as the little shyster's shoes hit the tile, he was gone. Looking over his shoulder and laughing at his mother, he made a mad dash around a potato chip display and headed straight for the ketchup aisle. I didn't see the chase, but I heard it. Everyone in the store heard it. Possibly everyone within a twenty-five-mile radius heard it. Finally, the mom came dragging her hostage back to the cart—he was kicking and screaming—and dumped him in.

Sadly, the line hadn't moved. I was still fourth. The little conniver and his mom were still third. And suddenly, it occurred to me that if I stood there and listened to that kid scream for one more minute, I might end up in jail. For life. So I gave up my place in line and walked out of the store.

I've reflected on that incident several times since then, and there's one thought that keeps throbbing in my brain. It's simply this: we start so early breaking our promises. That little boy couldn't have been more than three, but already he was a master manipulator who couldn't be trusted. I'd like to attribute his bad behavior to his age and say that someday he'll outgrow it, but I'd be a fool if I did. If I've learned anything in life, it's that adults are a thousand times more disingenuous than children.

I was reminded of this when a woman in our community told me that her husband had left her and their children for another woman. What made the situation unusually tragic was that the man had attended a big Promise Keepers crusade just three weeks before abandoning his family. The Sunday following the crusade, he wore his PK T-shirt to church and talked endlessly about the impact the event had had on his life.

Have you been lied to by someone you loved and thought you could trust? If so, that could be the reason why you're running low on faith. Nothing will turn your heart cold and bitter like the betrayal of a loved one. The pain stems not just from the betrayal itself but from the sudden fear that there's no one you can trust. Some people even grow suspicious of God. After all, if he's really in control, he could have stopped the betrayal from happening, right? Isn't the fact that he didn't a sort of betrayal?

I'm confident that a large percentage of the people reading this book are burn victims—people who've been burned by broken promises. If you're one of them, the last few paragraphs may already have your blood boiling as the memory of that experience comes rushing back. For the next few minutes, I invite you to join me in reflecting on our Lord's promises and his faithfulness. There are some vital truths that I believe will soothe your anger and refill your faith.

Faith Enough to Fish

The gentle, upward-sloping shores of the Sea of Galilee formed a natural amphitheater for any speaker standing at the water's edge. So it's not surprising that Jesus found himself there, looking up into the squinting, sun-scorched faces of people who'd heard amazing things about him and were anxious to find out if they could possibly be true. The crowd was large and, like most crowds, a bit unruly. The people pressed in, especially those in the back who were just on the edge of earshot.

I picture Jesus backing up, little by little, until he stood knee-deep in the water. With nowhere else to go, he turned to some fishermen who were washing their nets. One of them, a man named

Simon (who would later be called Peter) was kind enough to let Jesus stand in his boat. They pushed out a few feet from the shore, and Jesus continued teaching.

Little did Simon know that his life was about to change forever.

When Jesus finished teaching, he turned to Simon. Not to say thank you. Not to bid him farewell. Not to pay him for the use of his boat. No, he wanted to go fishing. In Luke 5:4, Jesus said to Simon, "Now go out where it is deeper and let down your nets, and you will catch many fish."

If you've got a rod and reel and a tackle box in your garage, you know that fishing is either the greatest activity in the world or the worst, depending on whether you're catching anything. If the fish are biting, you can cast and crank that monofilament all day. But if they're not, you'd just as soon have a wisdom tooth extracted.

Simon and his buddies were in no mood to do what Jesus was asking. They'd been at it all night and didn't have even a guppy to show for their efforts. They had almost all the seaweed and debris picked out of their nets and were ready for some sack time. Asking them to head back out into the deep at that moment would be like asking a short-order cook who's just gotten home from a ten-hour shift if he'd mind whipping up a few burgers. Further, Jesus wasn't exactly the Bass Pro Shop type. Sure, he was a gifted speaker, but what did he know about fishing? Simon and his cohorts were the pros. And tired pros at that. They had every right and reason to say to Jesus, "Sorry, Charlie. Maybe some other time."

But they didn't.

Instead, Simon, no doubt with a deep sigh and a roll of the eyes, said, "Master, we worked hard all last night and didn't catch a thing. But if you say so, we'll try again" (Luke 5:5).

I wonder if Jesus was able to keep the smirk off his face. He knew those crusty seamen were about to get their world, not to mention their boats, rocked. In a matter of minutes, their achy muscles were long forgotten as they struggled to pull in more fish than they'd ever seen before, let alone caught. Luke 5:7 says that both boats were so full of fish that they were on the verge of sinking.

Some people see nothing more than an odd coincidence in this story. They think Jesus just got lucky, or that he somehow spotted some movement in the water that indicated the arrival of a large school of fish. The one thing we know for certain is that Simon, who was an eyewitness and a seasoned fisherman, did not consider the catch a coincidence. His reaction indicates that he considered it a miracle. Luke 5:8, 9 says, "When Simon Peter realized what had happened, he fell to his knees before Jesus and said, 'Oh, Lord, please leave me—I'm too much of a sinner to be around you.' For he was awestruck by the size of their catch, as were the others with him."

Jesus had made a promise: "Let down your nets, and you will catch many fish" (v. 4). And they did. This was one of his earliest contacts with the men who would eventually be entrusted with the leadership of his church. The whole point of this miracle was to impress on them that he was someone who could be trusted. When he made a promise, they could count on its coming true. He would teach the lesson many more times, but this was one of the first. And it gives people who've been burned by broken promises plenty to think about. Let me offer three encouraging observations.

Every Promise Jesus Makes Has a Message

In 1970, George Zimmer graduated from Washington University in St. Louis, Missouri, with a degree in economics.[1] Three years later, he and his two college roommates opened the first Men's Wearhouse in Houston, Texas. Their inventory consisted mostly of polyester sport coats, and their technology was . . . well, nonexistent. Unable to afford a cash register, they kept their money and sales receipts in a cigar box.

In 1986, George made his first commercial. He stared into the camera and made the promise we've all become familiar with:

"You're going to like the way you look. I guarantee it." What most people don't know is that he goofed. He wasn't supposed to say "I guarantee it." He was supposed to say "That's the fact, Jack!" which would have been a takeoff on the catchphrase actor Bill Murray made popular in the movie *Stripes*.

It turned out to be a fortuitous accident.

That simple promise resonated with people and made them want to visit one of the stores. Today, Men's Wearhouse stores are all over the world, each year doing more than a billion dollars' worth of business. And George Zimmer is still guaranteeing that we're going to like the way we look.

That promise is not so different from the one Jesus made to Simon and his fishing partners.

On the surface, the promises seem completely different, one having to do with men's clothes and the other having to do with fish. But if you think about it, George is sending the same message to his potential customers that Jesus was sending to those weary fisherman: "You matter to me."

Jesus could have slapped those men on the back, thanked them for letting him use their boats, and walked away. They would have thought nothing of it. But his desire to hang out with them and his willingness to give them a huge payday told them that he cared about them.

This is the message in all great promises.

It's what a bride and groom are really saying to each other when they exchange their vows. It's what a parent means when he says to his child, "If you ever need to talk, I'll be here." It's what a young baby-toting wife means when she says to her departing GI husband, "I'll think of you every day." It's what a doctor means when he stares into the jaundiced eyes of a dying patient and says, "We'll do everything we can."

All great promises say "You matter to me."

That's what makes a broken promise so painful. Nothing hurts quite as badly as the realization that someone you trusted doesn't care after all.

If your faith needs refilling, I would recommend that you thumb through the Bible with a highlight marker in your hand and look for the promises Jesus made to you.

Here are a few to get you started:

- "Come to me, all of you who are weary and carry heavy burdens, and I will give you rest" (Matthew 11:28).
- "I assure you, everyone who has given up house or wife or brothers or parents or children, for the sake of the Kingdom of God, will be repaid many times over in this life, as well as receiving eternal life in the world to come" (Luke 18:29, 30).
- "I am the light of the world. If you follow me, you won't be stumbling through the darkness, because you will have the light that leads to life" (John 8:12).
- "All who are victorious will be clothed in white. I will never erase their names from the Book of Life, but I will announce before my Father and his angels that they are mine" (Revelation 3:5).

Woven into the fabric of these and many other promises is the simple message that our Lord cares about us. In spite of our failures, we matter to him. If we didn't, there would be no logical reason for him to make such commitments.

But not only is there a message in every promise . . .

EVERY PROMISE JESUS MAKES CONTAINS A CHALLENGE

The challenge will be to do something that goes against the grain, usually in one of three areas.

We are challenged to go against the grain of our feelings

That was the case with the disciples. They were exhausted after a long night of no-results fishing. They knew that shoving off again and heading for deep water would move their muscles from tired to full-blown ache status. But that was the only way to find out whether Jesus was the real deal or some kind of practical joker. They'd heard Jesus speak and were no doubt intrigued by his words, but only by doing what he asked would they find out if he was anything more than just a slick talker.

Right now, if your faith has bottomed out, you probably aren't feeling very spiritual. Maybe you've stopped praying, reading your Bible, or even going to church. You might get the occasional nudge, perhaps from a friend or an odd circumstance that triggers memories of happier times in your walk with the Lord. But I'm guessing that, so far, none of those nudges has been strong enough to overrule your feelings. This is a time for you to understand that your feelings will rob you of life's greatest blessings if you allow them to.

For some time now, I've been following a strict diet and exercise program. It's taken off my extra pounds, gotten my cholesterol down, and given me more strength and energy than I've had in years. The problem is, I have to exchange blows with my feelings several times a day. When I'm in a restaurant and a waiter strolls by my table with a big plate of cheese fries, I want to crawl after him on my hands and knees and bark like a dog. Or when I wake up at 6:00 AM and hear the exercise bike calling me from the other room, I want to hunker down under the covers and put my fingers in my ears. I'm not kidding when I say that if I allowed my feelings to dictate my actions, I'd weigh three hundred pounds and would be a heart attack or stroke waiting to happen. I'd never know the blessing of good health.

The same is true in the spiritual realm. You have to go against the grain of your feelings if you ever hope to see God's promises come true in your life. They will generally require something of you that you won't always feel like doing, like going the extra mile.

Or turning the other cheek.

Or casting a net one more time when all you want to do is crash.

WE ARE CHALLENGED TO GO AGAINST THE GRAIN OF OUR RELATIONSHIPS

In Matthew 19:29, Jesus said, "Everyone who has given up houses or brothers or sisters or father or mother or children or property, for my sake, will receive a hundred times as much in return and will have eternal life."

Every time I read that promise, my eyes go straight to the phrase "a hundred times as much." I was never worth a hoot at math, but I know enough to know that you can take just about any crooked number and multiply it by one hundred and have a whole lot more than you started out with. It's easy to love the second half of that verse.

But the first half isn't as appealing.

Not by a long shot.

It reminds us that our Lord's promises sometimes require us to make excruciating relationship choices.

I once knew a young woman who grew up in another religion. Her family was very narrow-minded and intolerant, especially when it came to matters of faith. Her parents told her flat out that if she were baptized into Christ, they would disown her. The poor woman sat in our living room on a Thursday night and sobbed as she told Marilyn and me about her predicament. We read Matthew 19:29 together and talked and prayed. The following Sunday, in what I consider to be one of the greatest acts of courage I've ever witnessed, the young woman accepted Christ and was immersed. As we expected, her parents and siblings were irate and hatefully refused her invitation to attend the service. I'm happy to report that they eventually did come around, somewhat. But when the young woman made her decision, she believed she was giving up her family for Jesus' sake. I can still remember her poignant observation that being repaid a hundred times over sounds pretty good when you're talking about money, but it seems like a small consolation when you're losing your family.

WE ARE CHALLENGED TO GO AGAINST THE GRAIN OF OUR CULTURE

Who are some of the biggest influencers in American culture? One would be shock-radio host Howard Stern. Sirius satellite radio invested 100 million dollars to acquire exclusive rights to his radio program. Howard Stern said, "I'm sickened by all religions. Religion has divided people. I don't think there's any difference between the pope wearing a large hat and parading around with a smoking purse and an African painting his face white and praying to a rock."[2]

Another cultural icon is Brad Pitt. You can't walk through a grocery store checkout line without seeing his face on half a dozen magazines. The world seems obsessed with his every move. Brad Pitt said with regard to religion, "I would call it oppression because it stifles any kind of personal individual freedom."[3]

And then there is Oprah Winfrey. Who's had a bigger impact on American culture than she has? She was added to the Forbes billionaire list in 2003 and continues to expand her power base. She's so influential she can turn an obscure book into an instant mega best seller simply by giving it her stamp of approval. Some have even spoken of the "Oprahfication" of America. But when asked about God, she said, "One of the biggest mistakes humans make is to believe there is only one way. Actually, there are many diverse paths leading to what you call God."[4]

With these people (and hundreds of others just like them) holding so much power in America, is it any wonder our culture has become so warped? Sadly, it's against the rushing current of that culture that you and I must live. Every choice we make for God will be met with a roll of the eyes and a shake of the head. We'll be pitied, laughed at, and dismissed as lunatics for putting our faith in God's promises. This is why Jesus said, "God blesses you when you are mocked and persecuted and lied about because you are my followers. Be happy about it! Be very glad! For a great reward awaits you in heaven" (Matthew 5:11, 12).

Take any promise our Lord ever made, and you'll find in it a message and a challenge. But here's the best news:

EVERY PROMISE JESUS MAKES COMES WITH A BLESSING

If you have the courage to meet the challenge of the promise, you will receive the blessing of the promise. The disciples mustered up enough willpower to row out into the deep and cast those nets one more time. They ended up with two boatloads of fish (literally!) and an experience they would never forget.

Some of God's promises contain a physical blessing, but *all* of them contain a spiritual blessing. In the account we've just studied, the promise Jesus made contained both a physical *and* a spiritual blessing. In addition to the record catch, the disciples also were blessed with powerful glimpses of Jesus' power and trustworthiness. Which blessing had the bigger impact on their lives? It was obviously the spiritual blessing, for they "left everything and followed Jesus" (Luke 5:11). Or maybe they did so because they knew they would eat well!

As a minister, I frequently run into people who've become bitter toward God because they feel unblessed. A common remark they make is, "I see God doing things for other people, but he's never done anything for me." My response is that God may have done more for them than they give him credit for. Further, I try to lovingly point out that if the person feels blessing deprived, there is a surefire way to fix the problem. Just start meeting the challenges contained in our Lord's promises. No one has ever been faithful to God without God being faithful in return. Read Hebrews 6:18

carefully: "God has given us both his promise and his oath. These two things are unchangeable because it is impossible for God to lie. Therefore, we who have fled to him for refuge can take new courage, for we can hold on to his promise with confidence."

If you're running low on faith, it's probably been a while since you've really taken God's promises seriously. Maybe a period of testing sparked some doubts about him, and you lost your enthusiasm for obedience. Let me encourage you to wrap your heart around Hebrews 6:18 and try again. Put God to the test, and see if he will deliver on his promises.

He will. I guarantee it.

And when he does, you're going to like the way it looks. And maybe kick yourself for doubting him. Most importantly, you'll feel a fresh, warm, stream of faith flowing into your empty heart.

topping it off

1. *Nothing will turn your heart cold and bitter like the betrayal of a loved one. The pain stems not just from the betrayal itself but from the sudden fear that there's no one you can trust. Some people even grow suspicious of God. After all, if he's really in control, he could have stopped the betrayal from happening, right? Isn't the fact that he didn't a sort of betrayal?* Do you consider it a betrayal on God's part when he doesn't protect you from being hurt? Have you ever become angry at God because of what another person did? How did you deal with that?

2. *You have to go against the grain of your feelings if you ever hope to see God's promises come true in your life.* When have your feelings kept you from claiming one of God's promises? How did you overcome those feelings?

3. *In Matthew 19:29, Jesus said, "Everyone who has given up houses or brothers or sisters or father or mother or children or property, for my sake, will receive a hundred times as much in return and will have eternal life."* Have you ever been forced to give up a human relationship to save your relationship with God? How difficult was it for you to make that decision? How did you feel blessed for doing so?

4. *As a minister, I frequently run into people who've become bitter toward God because they feel unblessed. A common remark they make is, "I see God doing things for other people, but he's never done anything for me."* Have you ever felt that way? What are the flaws in that kind of attitude? What are some things you could do to make yourself more sensitive to God's blessings?

5
REFILLING YOUR FAITH IN HIS LOVE

JOHN 13:1-17

*Maybe the reason we've not felt God's affection more is that
we've been too bashful to call Jesus the Lover of our souls. We've
worshiped God as the Creator who owns the cosmos. We've
proclaimed Him the King who rules the world. We've called
on Him as the Father who cares for His children. But we've
been too coy about the Groom who rejoices over His bride.*

—ALAN D. WRIGHT

Superman has always been my favorite superhero. Disguised in
his off-hours as the mild-mannered reporter Clark Kent, Superman
has been busting bad guys since before I was born. As a little boy, I
used to tie a bath towel around my neck and park myself in front of
an old black-and-white TV to watch the George Reeves version of
my hero do his thing. In every episode, at a moment of high drama
(at least it seemed high to a five-year-old), he ripped off those nerdy
glasses and ducked into the *Daily Planet* storeroom. That's when I
jumped to my feet and scurried up onto the arm of the sofa. Seconds
later, just when Superman leaped out the storeroom window to
the accompaniment of a rapturous musical fanfare, I would launch
myself with a war whoop off the sofa, landing with a thud in the
middle of the living room floor. It was awesome!

So you can imagine my excitement when I realized that some
brilliant, insightful TV producers had decided to launch a new

Superman series. *Smallville* is the story of Clark Kent's life as a high-school student. As you would expect, he's a great kid. He's respectful toward his parents, possesses strong values, makes good grades, and uses his budding superpowers to foil every fiendish plot that comes down the pike. There's only one thing about the show that bothers me: Clark can't ever seem to get together with the girl he loves.

Lana Lang is everything a high-school boy would want in a girlfriend. Drop-dead gorgeous, wholesome, drop-dead gorgeous, sweet, drop-dead gorgeous, intelligent, and drop-dead gorgeous. What frustrates me is that they adore each other, but for some inexplicable reason, Clark is never able to embrace that fact. They have times when they grow very close, but then something happens and Clark pulls away. He begins to doubt his worthiness, or Lana's feelings, in spite of the fact that she does everything she can to show him she loves him.

Sound familiar?

This is the pattern that most Christians follow in their walks with the Lord. God loves us, but much of the time we have trouble embracing that fact. When some terrible twist of circumstances comes into our lives, we pull away, wondering how a loving God could allow such a thing to happen. Or when we stumble and fall into sin, we pull away, assuming that a holy God could only be disgusted with us. The result is that we never really get to know and enjoy God's love the way he intends for us to. Suspicion or guilt always seems to stand in our way.

And let's face it. There is no misery greater than feeling unloved. If you have ever been abandoned by a parent, betrayed by a spouse, or dumped by the girl or guy of your dreams, you know this all too well. I've watched strong, capable men and women crumble under the anguish of a lost love, and the agony can be even worse when you don't feel loved by God.

Just before I started to write this chapter, I opened an e-mail from a reader who told me the story of how, after many years of living for herself, she finally gave her life to Christ. She was giddy with excitement and determined to spend every day of the rest of her life serving her Lord. Then, just a few weeks after her conversion, she was diagnosed with terminal cancer and given only a few months to live. Can you blame her for turning her face toward Heaven and screaming, "OK, God, what's up with this? I give *you* my heart and you give *me* cancer!"

Right now, does your faith in God's love need a refill? Is there something—perhaps pain or guilt—that makes you wonder where you really stand with him? If so, join me in a journey back to John 13, where we find Jesus teaching an unforgettable lesson about his love.

Twenty-four Feet of Love

Chapters 13 through 17 of the Gospel of John are known as the Farewell Discourse. They contain Jesus' last words and tell about his final interactions with his disciples. The moments described are very poignant, as you would expect. When you know you're about to die—that your days are dwindling down to hours—every word and action will surely be significant and packed with emotion. It doesn't matter if you're talking about jelly beans or minutes spent with a loved one. When you know they're about to run out, you start savoring every one.

As John 13 opens, we're told that Jesus set out to show his disciples "the full extent of his love" (v. 1). I find significance in the word "show" in that verse. Jesus, in his wisdom, understood that just telling his disciples about the full extent of his love wouldn't cut it. He knew, as we all do, that professions of love are as common as mosquitoes in July. He also must have believed that actions speak louder than words . . . that a demonstration would stick with them longer than a declaration. So after the disciples assumed their places around the table, Jesus took off his robe, wrapped a towel around his waist, poured water into a basin, and prepared to wash their feet.

Leonardo da Vinci once observed that "the foot is a masterpiece of engineering and a work of art."[1] If you're barefooted as you're reading this, move the book aside and take a look at your tootsies. Of the 206 bones in your body, 52 of them are right there in your feet. They are connected by 66 joints, moved by 40 muscles, and held together by 200 ligaments. Each foot also houses an intricate network of nerves and blood vessels. God even provided little sheaths of protective armor (also known as toenails) to protect the tips of your toes. So Leo was right. The foot *is* a masterpiece of engineering and a work of art. No wonder the largest and strongest tendon in the foot is named after an ancient Greek hero.

On the other hand, the foot is not exactly the most attractive part of the human body. And why would it be? During the typical day, your feet endure the cumulative force of several hundred tons. That's during the *typical* day. On days when you go to the mall or walk the golf course, the pounding your feet suffer is multiplied many times over. And often this pounding is administered while our feet are stuffed into shoes that are too big, too small, or too stupidly designed to be of any comfort. I dare say you couldn't put any part of your body through that kind of abuse and have it come out looking beautiful.

There's also the fact that your feet can suffer a variety of maladies. Corns, calluses, cracked heels, ingrown toenails, bunions, warts, and rashes are not only painful but can make your feet horrifying to look at. And that's not to mention the smell. The reason feet stink is because they contain approximately two hundred fifty thousand sweat glands that can secrete as much as half a pint of moisture per day. (Give the Odor-Eaters people credit. They have parlayed one of the most inglorious facts about the human body into a fortune.)

But however unattractive modern feet are, feet had to be even worse in Bible times. Imagine people walking everywhere on dusty roads that were traveled by donkeys and other animals. People were either barefooted or in sandals—and did not have a nail salon to retreat to for a pedicure, or John Madden to tell them about tough actin' Tinactin.

The disciples undoubtedly had some seriously nasty feet under those robes. So when it became clear that Jesus intended to wash them, it's not surprising that he met with some resistance. Peter, for one, had no intention of letting Jesus wash his feet. John 13:8 says that he "protested." I don't blame him. I would've too. If you ever walk up to me and volunteer to wash my feet, expect to be turned down. That's something I can do for myself, thank you very much.

But this washing exercise wasn't just about hygiene. It was a teaching opportunity. Jesus was showing the disciples the extent of his love for them. And for you and me. Notice three great truths that I'm certain will refill your faith in his love.

Our Filth Doesn't Diminish Jesus' Love for Us

When Jesus gently lifted those ugly, stinking feet and rinsed and dried them with the loving care of a mother bathing her newborn baby, he was showing his disciples that he could stomach their filth. But not just that he *could* stomach it. He was showing them that he *would* stomach it. This is an important distinction.

There are a lot of things in this world I *could* do, but that I *wouldn't* do unless someone was holding a gun to my head. For example, since we're on the subject of feet, www.foothealthcare.com reports that the world record for most feet sniffed belongs to Madeline Albrecht of Cincinnati, Ohio. Madeline works for a research company that tests Dr. Scholl's foot care products. At the time of the report, she had sniffed five thousand six hundred feet. You can't even imagine how hungry I'd have to be before I took a job like that.

For most people, *could* and *would* are two different things. But not for Jesus. He *can* stomach our filth, and he *will*.

The Bible teaches this truth through many dramatic stories, but my favorite is found in the book of Hosea. Alan D. Wright, in his book *Lover of My Soul*, sets up the story with profound insight and a gentle wit:

> The young evangelist, a highly eligible bachelor and powerful preacher, attracted the attention of the church ladies. Many women may have hoped for a date with the nationally known communicator, but everyone knew he wouldn't marry until God told him when—and who.
>
> I imagine he, like all men, thought about getting married. I'm sure he wanted to feel a woman's affection, longed for a partner who would share his life and his vision, wanted a helpmate to walk through the valleys with him and to smile as together they navigated the precipices. I'm sure he prayed that God would give him a wonderful wife.
>
> Then one day out of the blue, God spoke to the preacher. *It's time for you to get married. I have selected you a wife.*
>
> Like an exuberant child, the man of God thrust his fist in the air, did a little victory dance, and shouted, "YES!"
>
> "Who is it, Lord?" the preacher began to ponder. "Is it Samantha in the choir? The one with the beautiful voice—ahh, what a sweet melody comes from her mouth. Is she the one, Lord? I could make beautiful harmony with her."
>
> *No. She is not in the choir.*
>
> "Oh well," the minister conceded. "Is it Mary Jo, the new secretary? I don't know her very well yet, but she's beautiful, and I know she's a good administrator. I could use a wife with a good sense of details. Is it she?"
>
> *No. She is not in the church at all.*
>
> "Not in the church? Oh, she's in another church. Okay, I can handle that. What denomination is she? Is it that woman with the red hair I met at the Christian bookstore the other day?"
>
> *No, she's not in any church.*

"What do you mean, Lord, 'not in any church'? Where would she be? Where might I find her then?"

Go downtown, past the old depot, next to the abandoned warehouse. You'll see an old store with a red light that says "All Girl Staff." She's in there.

The preacher grew silent. Surely he hadn't heard God correctly. "Lord, my future wife couldn't be there. That's the worst part of town!"

She's there.

"But Lord, I can't even be seen in a place like that! It's a house of ill repute. It's a brothel! What would the parishioners say if they found out I'd gone there? What would my future wife be doing in a brothel? Is she a missionary? A social worker? What is she?"

She's a harlot. Now, "Go, take to yourself an adulterous wife."[2]

It's true. God told the prophet Hosea to marry a prostitute. If you don't believe me, read it for yourself in Hosea 1:2. The question is, why? Why would God want one of his right-hand men to marry one of the filthiest women in town? Simple. So Hosea could understand in some small way what it was like for God to be in a relationship with the people of Israel.

Can you imagine yourself marrying a prostitute? Or if you're a woman, can you imagine yourself marrying a pimp with a dozen girls under his control? or a drug pusher? or a rapist?

Of course you can't. The idea disgusts you. But you'd *have* to do such a thing if you ever wanted to fully appreciate what God has done. Through his Son, he has reached out his hand to every filthy, wretched sinner in this world and said, "I love you, and I want to have a relationship with you." He wouldn't do that if he couldn't stomach our filth.

Let's go back to John 13 for a moment.

Has it ever occurred to you that two of the twenty-four feet Jesus washed that night belonged to the man who would betray him into the hands of murderers just hours later? Yes, Judas—Mr. Thirty Pieces of Silver—was there among the twelve. Who would have dreamed that there was something more nasty and gross at that table than the disciples' feet? But there was, and it was Judas's heart. Imagine how awkward he must have felt when Jesus pushed the basin toward him and looked up into his eyes. Was he expecting Jesus to skip him and move on to the next person or perhaps dump the water over his head? If so, he got a surprise. Jesus bathed his feet with the same loving care he gave to Peter and John.

This should be a tremendous encouragement to you if you've been thinking that maybe God can't stomach you because of the sins you've committed. Of course, he hates your sin, and he hates even more what it does to you. But not for an instant could your sin ever cause his love to waver. The apostle Paul said that nothing can ever separate us from his love (Romans 8:38). That includes the filth in your life and mine.

Here's another great truth:

OUR RESISTANCE DOESN'T DIMINISH JESUS' LOVE FOR US

Have you ever loved someone who didn't love you back?

When I was in high school, I had a couple of dates with a girl who never should have looked twice at me. I was a skinny, gangly kid with braces, and even worse, I was a band geek. The girl, on the other hand, was all blond and beautiful, a cheerleader, and the object of every male student's fantasies. In what was for me a pleasant twist of circumstances, we were thrown together in the same classes and became friends almost from the first day of school. It didn't take me long to develop a crush the size of the Golden Gate Bridge, and, believe it or not, the record shows that we had two official dates.

But it became apparent that she wasn't as smitten with me as I was with her. I suspected as much when she started resisting all of my ideas for how we could spend more time together. But the dead giveaway was when I started seeing her walking the halls with guys who weren't band geeks. Guys who didn't have biceps the size of broom handles and didn't have metal in their mouths.

I won't say I wasn't brokenhearted when the stone-cold realization hit me that we weren't meant to be together. But I can honestly say the heartbreak didn't last long. There's something about having your advances resisted that makes it easy to move on.

For you and me maybe, but not for Jesus.

When Jesus knelt before Peter and prepared to wash his feet, he met with some serious resistance. Peter protested, saying, "No, you will never wash my feet!" It's impossible to say why he was so adamant. Surely he felt that such a job was beneath Jesus. Or maybe his feet were unusually ugly, dirty, or diseased. Or it might have had something to do with Peter's pride. Whatever the case, he wanted nothing to do with Jesus' expression of love and tenderness.

If I'd been in Jesus' position, I would have thrown my hands into the air and said, "OK, OK . . . no need to get upset. If you don't want me to wash your feet, I'll just skip you and move on."

But Jesus wasn't put off by Peter's resistance.

He never is.

This is one of the greatest facts about our Lord. We can avoid, defy, elude, evade, rebuff, resist, or reject him, but it doesn't change the way he feels about us. Nor does it diminish his desire to bless us.

In Revelation 3:20, Jesus said, "Look! Here I stand at the door and knock. If you hear me calling and open the door, I will come in, and we will share a meal as friends." A thousand vacuum cleaner salesmen put together would never encounter as many slammed doors as Jesus does. Yet, in every case, he keeps knocking and calling out in a tender, friendly voice, hoping only for a chance to demonstrate his love.

In Psalm 139:7, 8, David said, "I can never escape from your spirit! I can never get away from your presence! If I go up to heaven, you are there; if I go down to the place of the dead, you are there." Question: Why would someone go down to the place of the dead, if not in an effort to get away from God? Yet, even there in the darkness, he bumps into the Almighty. We see in these verses an *accompanying* God, a God who goes with us wherever we go. But perhaps we also ought to see in them a *pursuing* God, a God who follows us wherever we go because he can't stand the thought of losing us.

Remember Jonah?

God asked him to become a missionary to wicked Nineveh. That would be like asking an American minister today to go to the Middle East and preach to Hamas or al-Qaeda. Jonah did what a lot of us would do. He took off in the opposite direction. But God followed him. Throughout the book of Jonah, we see God manipulating Jonah's surroundings—creating storms and controlling fish—all because he loved Jonah too much to let him go. Even though Jonah resisted him big time, God continued to pursue him.

Many who read this book will be able to tell similar stories of how our Lord pursued them, wooed them, and eventually overcame their resistance. Maybe you can think of a time when you tried to flee from God, but found that he wouldn't leave you alone. Every day, some little incident—a song, a news report, a conversation, a chance meeting with an old friend—reminded you of his love and made you homesick, eventually causing you to give up the fugitive life and go home. I have a friend who says he's tried to run away from God six times in his life, and every time God has tracked him down.

Clearly, our filth doesn't diminish his love for us, and neither does our resistance.

And finally . . .

Our Cluelessness Doesn't Diminish Jesus' Love for Us

When you read the account of Jesus washing the disciples' feet, you see so clearly the gap that existed between what he was trying to teach and what they were able to grasp. Peter asked point-blank, "Lord, why are you going to wash my feet?" And Jesus answered, "You don't understand now why I am doing it; someday you will" (John 13:6, 7).

I have a confession to make: clueless people drive me nuts. I don't mind if someone has a good reason for being clueless. I can handle a child who's being exposed to something new for the first time, or a new employee struggling through his first day on a new job. No problem at all. But when a person has had plenty of opportunities to get a clue and still doesn't get it, I become really frustrated.

Think about the disciples. Jesus had been mentoring them for almost three years. They'd been traveling with him, listening to him preach, and watching him handle his adversaries almost on a daily basis. Yet they still had very little understanding of what his purpose was. Even when Jesus spoke to them in explicit terms, they still had trouble connecting the dots. I can only assume that, at times, Jesus must have been frustrated out of his mind. I can almost picture him with his face in his hands, shaking his head, wondering how in the world he managed to end up with such bozos. Surely the words of Isaiah 1:3 must have echoed through his mind: "Even the animals—the donkey and the ox—know their owner and appreciate his care, but not my people Israel. No matter what I do for them, they still do not understand."

But then two thoughts quickly come to mind.

First, I realize that there are times when I'm pretty clueless too. Sometimes I say and do things that only a moron would say and do. Just last week, I had to apologize to a wonderful member of our church for a lamebrain comment I made that was very hurtful to her. Looking back, I can't believe I was so thoughtless and insensitive

. . . but I was. So I really don't have any room to talk about others who might be clueless.

Second, I realize how incredible Jesus is for putting up with our brain cramps, our foolishness, and our failure to grasp the obvious . . . and loving us anyway. That *can't* be easy. What *would* be easy is for him to say "That's it. I've had enough!"

Many years ago, when my daughter Michelle was a toddler, she climbed out of bed very early one Saturday morning and made her way to the kitchen. While her mother and I slept, she pulled open the refrigerator door and found herself staring at a full carton of fresh eggs. To her, they must have looked like little balls. I assume that, because she promptly started picking them up one at a time and trying to bounce them on the tile floor.

Down the hall in the master bedroom, Marilyn was awakened by an unusual sound.

Splat . . . splat . . . splat.

It took a moment for the sound to cut through the fog of sleep and register in her mind, but when it did she bolted upright and shook me awake.

"Listen!" she said.

Splat . . . splat . . . splat.

Suddenly, we were throwing covers left and right and flying out of bed. We raced down the hall and rounded the corner into the kitchen, only to find Michelle in her jammies, grinning ear to ear, playing in a gooey pool of broken eggs. I'm sure she thought we had come to join in the fun. She was not happy when she realized that was not the case.

Thinking back, I remember how filthy she was, all covered in egg goo. She was also resistant to my efforts to clean her up— wiggling, squirming, and whining as I wiped the goo away. But most of all, she was clueless. She couldn't begin to understand why I was ruining what had been, for her, a cracking good time.

Filthy, resistant, and *clueless.*

That was my daughter in a nutshell . . . or perhaps I should say in an eggshell.

But not for one instant did I stop loving her.

And the Lord won't stop loving you either, even if you make a mess of your life. John 1:17 says, "God's unfailing love and faithfulness came through Jesus Christ."

"Unfailing."

That word makes all the difference, doesn't it?

topping it off

1. *I've watched strong, capable men and women crumble under the anguish of a lost love, and the agony can be even worse when you don't feel loved by God.* Have you ever questioned God's love for you? What circumstances caused you to do that? Do you still feel that way? If not, how did you overcome those feelings?

2. *Who would have dreamed that there was something more nasty and gross at that table than the disciples' feet? But there was, and it was Judas's heart. Imagine how awkward he must have felt when Jesus pushed the basin toward him and looked up into his eyes. . . . Jesus bathed his feet with the same loving care he gave to Peter and John.* What do you think was going through Jesus' mind as he knelt before Judas? What do you think was going through Judas's mind? Have you ever had to minister to someone you considered to be an enemy? How did it feel? If you've never had to, do you think you'd be able if the situation arose?

3. *Many who read this book will be able to tell similar stories of how our Lord pursued them, wooed them, and eventually overcame their resistance.* Can you tell such a story? Why were you resisting God, and how did he overcome your resistance?

4. *I realize how incredible Jesus is for putting up with our brain cramps, our foolishness, and our failure to grasp the obvious . . . and loving us anyway. That* can't *be easy.* Can you think of a truth or a lesson that you were slow to learn? What finally triggered the realization in your mind? What effect has your experience had on your attitude toward clueless people in your world?

6
REFILLING YOUR FAITH IN HIS GOODNESS

JOHN 11:1-44

I am a candidate for conversion. Bring me something better than Jesus and his way, and I'll take it.

—E. STANLEY JONES

Have you ever had someone get in your face and tell you what a terrible person you are? I have. More than once, actually.

One time was when a couple in their late twenties asked me to perform their wedding ceremony. The bride-to-be was a Christian. But her fiancé was not and, in fact, made no secret of his apathy toward God and Christianity. So I did what I always do in that situation. As gently and politely as possible, I read and explained the Bible's instruction that Christians should avoid becoming unequally yoked. Further, I pointed out that my calling wasn't to perform wedding ceremonies but to help establish and build Christian homes. They received my words as graciously as I spoke them, and we parted on good terms.

Or so I thought.

About half an hour later, the woman's father came bursting into my office with all the finesse of a SWAT team commander trying to capture an al-Qaeda terrorist. To say he was offended by my refusal to perform his daughter's wedding ceremony would be like saying the pope is a little put off by Howard Stern's humor. For ten minutes he screamed at me. He told me I was a pitiful excuse for a minister. He said it was because of idiots like me that so many people hate the church. (Yes, he really said "idiots.") In the middle of it all, he even slammed his fist down on my desk, causing the head on my St. Louis Cardinals bobblehead to start bouncing up and down. I remember thinking that it looked as if the doll were nodding in agreement with everything the man was saying. The little traitor!

When things like that happen, I find comfort in the fact that far better men than I have suffered similar indignities. For example, in 2 Samuel 16, there's an account of King David and his men passing by the village of Bahurim. Suddenly, a man named Shimei came running toward them, cursing and throwing stones. Come to find out, he was one of Saul's relatives and was still sore because Saul had lost his throne to David. It wasn't David's fault. In fact, he'd had opportunities to kill Saul, but refused. Shimei either didn't know that or didn't care. In his mind, David was the devil himself. "Get out of here, you murderer, you scoundrel!" he screamed (v. 7).

As you might expect, David's right-hand man begged for permission to lop off Shimei's head with a sword and shut him up for good. But David, in an amazing show of restraint, refused to grant it. Instead, he allowed the man to walk alongside their party, hurling insults, cursing, and throwing stones.

But of all the people who've ever had their goodness unfairly called into question, no one stands out more than Jesus. Hebrews 4:15 says he was without sin. Acts 10:38 says that he "went around doing good and healing all who were oppressed by the Devil." Even Pilate failed to find a flaw in Jesus' life, according to John 18:38. But that didn't stop some people from pegging him as a bad guy. For example, in Luke 23 he was accused of leading people to ruin (v. 2), of causing riots (v. 5), and of being an insurrectionist (v. 14). People were so convinced he was a criminal that they screamed for him to be killed (v. 18).

I'm pretty sure you've never thought of Jesus in such harsh terms. But I wonder if there have been times when you couldn't help thinking that Jesus might not be quite as good as you've been led to believe. Maybe you prayed hard about some difficult problem and got no discernible response. Perhaps a torrent of trouble came flooding into your life, and you feel that he could have—and *should* have—prevented it. Or maybe there was a time when his requirements and instructions seemed oppressive and unreasonable.

These are the kinds of experiences that cause second thoughts about our Lord's goodness to sprout in our minds. And once they sprout, Satan does everything in his power to water and fertilize them. In fact, you may have noticed that Satan invests very little time and energy trying to convince us that God is bad. He knows that's a hard sell. Too hard, in most cases. So he chooses instead to fill our minds with suspicion.

Remember the Garden of Eden?

The serpent didn't bother trying to convince Eve that God was an evil monster. He merely suggested that God wasn't being entirely honest about why he instructed her and Adam not to eat the fruit that was growing on the tree in the middle of the garden. He said, "God knows that your eyes will be opened when you eat it. You will become just like God, knowing everything, both good and evil" (Genesis 3:5). Do you see the subtle implication? *God isn't bad, exactly. He just isn't quite as good as you thought.* Satan knows that when that idea sinks its roots into your mind, the draining of your faith will begin in earnest. From that point on, every time something bad happens, you'll throw a suspicious glare in the Lord's direction.

If second thoughts about our Lord's goodness have started sprouting in your mind, I encourage you to take a look at the powerful account of Lazarus's resurrection from the dead in John 11. This well-known story is a testimony about our Lord's power, but it is just as much a story about his goodness.

From Here to Eternity . . . and Back

One day, Jesus was approached by two messengers who'd been sent from the little town of Bethany by his friends Mary and Martha. Obviously, Jesus knew what they were going to say before they said it. But even if he hadn't, he probably would have been able to guess from the expressions on their faces that the news was grim. And indeed it was. The messengers reported that Lazarus, Mary and Martha's brother and one of Jesus' closest friends, was gravely ill. The original language suggests that he was going down quickly.

In truth, he probably was already dead.

In his book *Jesus According to Scripture*, Darrell Bock analyzes the timing of the passage and suggests that Lazarus was alive when the messengers left to go find Jesus, but died before they found him.[1] They, of course, wouldn't have known this, but Jesus did. That's why he said, "Lazarus's sickness will not end in death" (John 11:4). The key word is "end." Jesus didn't promise that Lazarus wouldn't die, only that death wouldn't be the *end* of the story. And it wasn't.

Jesus eventually made his way to Lazarus's tomb, where he performed a miracle so incredible that it's familiar even to people who've never read a word of Scripture. With three simple words—"Lazarus, come out!" (v. 43)—Jesus broke the hammerlock death held on his friend. You can be sure some serious gasps and bug eyes greeted Lazarus as he staggered out of the tomb, struggling against the linen wrappings that bound him from head to toe. But something tells me Lazarus's own eyes were the widest of them all. The man had been on one of the most amazing journeys any human has ever traveled: from here to eternity . . . and back!

Years ago, a man who'd just started attending our church made an appointment to speak with me. Usually, I know what people want to talk about before I meet with them, but somehow this guy managed to get on my docket without revealing that information. As he walked into my office, I sized him up. He was well dressed, friendly, and articulate. I had no reason to suspect anything weird was about to happen, but it was.

We engaged in small talk for a few minutes, and finally I said, "How can I help you?" His response was that *he* intended to help *me*, which was when the first red flag went up. I'd heard those words before, which is why the terms *multilevel marketing* and *pyramid scheme* suddenly popped into my mind. At that moment, I fully expected him to start telling me how selling toothpaste and laundry detergent was going to change my life. But he didn't. Instead, he said he wanted to share his experiences with me because he knew they would help me as a pastor.

That's when the second red flag went up.

It struck me that you have to be pretty cocky to tell someone you don't even know that you can help him do his job better. I might have felt differently if he'd been a retired minister or if he'd been hawking some sort of leadership seminar or video series. But no, he readily admitted that he'd never been to seminary or worked one day in the ministry. He also assured me that he didn't have a product to sell. He only said that his experiences were going to help me. Trying not to sound as skeptical as I felt, I asked, "What experiences are you referring to?"

"I've died and gone to Heaven twice," he said.

Suddenly, multilevel marketing didn't sound so bad.

"Oh really?" was all I could think of to say.

"Yes, I'm a modern-day Lazarus," he said, and, sadly, I could tell he was serious.

But of course, he *wasn't* a modern-day Lazarus. He was just a guy with a long history of emotional problems who was starved for attention.

The historical account of Lazarus's death and resurrection bears no resemblance to the so-called after-life experiences that many people today claim to have had. John 11:17 says that Lazarus spent four days in a grave. There are many instances on record of people reviving after being left for dead, pronounced dead, or zipped up in a body bag. But when was the last time you heard about someone being resurrected after spending four days in a grave? Without embalming or air-conditioning, ninety-six hours would put a cadaver so far into the decaying process that even the most jaded horror movie buff would be repulsed. This is why Martha, Lazarus's sister, warned Jesus that opening her brother's tomb would release foul odors into the air (v. 39).

Let me be clear. I'm placing no limits on God's power. He can raise anybody he wants anytime he wants. But when you hear someone claim to be a modern-day Lazarus, you should be more than a little skeptical. The world is full of con artists and nutcases. The raising of Lazarus is one of our Lord's greatest miracles, accomplished to show the world what resurrection power looks like and to lend credibility to his promises. What I love is that it also puts his goodness on display.

Jesus' Relationships Demonstrated His Goodness

Jesus and the three siblings, Mary, Martha, and Lazarus, shared a special bond that was probably first established when Jesus and his disciples needed a place to stay and were welcomed into their home (Luke 10:38). Obviously, they saw goodness in Jesus because you would never welcome someone into your home if you thought he was bad. But they also must have sensed that Jesus was a down-to-earth guy . . . that his goodness wasn't so pompous that they would be uncomfortable having him around.

There are two kinds of goodness: the cold kind and the warm kind. For example, there's the kind of goodness that is all about propriety. It requires you to sit up straight, put both feet on the floor, chew with your mouth shut, and eat your chicken with a knife and fork. But there's also the kind of goodness that lets you tuck a napkin into your shirt, plant your elbows on the table, and eat your chicken with your fingers. No doubt you know very good people who fit both descriptions. Around the former group you feel a little tense, like you have to be constantly on guard lest you make a mistake that might offend somebody's sense of decorum. But around the latter group you can relax and be yourself.

There are numerous indications in Scripture that Jesus' goodness was the warm kind. For example, think about his first encounter with Levi, who later became known as Matthew. Remember how, after just one conversation, Levi walked away from his life as a crooked tax collector and became a disciple? (Matthew 9:9). If Jesus had been cold, that never would have happened. And what about the fact that Levi then invited all of his shady friends over to meet Jesus that very night? (v. 10). If our Lord had come off as being rigid, legalistic, or holier-than-thou, do you think he would have done that? Perhaps the greatest indication that our Lord's goodness is the down-to-earth variety is the fact that he became known as a friend of sinners (Luke 7:34).

In our world, a good example of this kind of goodness is Tony Dungy, the head football coach of the Indianapolis Colts. No one in public life puts forth a more disciplined Christian witness, as the whole world saw in the 2005–06 NFL play-offs. At the end of a hotly contested play-off game against the underdog Pittsburgh Steelers, Colts kicker Mike Vangerjagt botched what would have been a game-tying field goal. It was a crushing, season-ending mistake that would have sent many coaches off on a profanity-laced tirade. But not Tony Dungy. The cameras were tight on his face when the ball sailed wide of the upright. Ever the gentleman, he simply winced and said, "He missed it."

But game-related tests are the least of what Tony Dungy's faith has been subjected to. You may recall that just a few days before Christmas in 2005, Tony's eighteen-year-old son, James, hanged himself from a ceiling fan in his Tampa apartment. It was the kind of emotional trauma that sends even the staunchest of believers into a deep, spiritual funk. But Tony stood firm in his faith and, in a move that almost blows my mind, delivered a powerful, faith-filled sermon at his son's funeral.

But as good as he is, Tony Dungy is still warm and engaging. People who have nothing in common with him spiritually still feel drawn to him. It's common to hear some of the worldliest, most potty-mouthed NFL players speak glowingly of their love and respect for him.

You see, the thing about warmth is that it causes things to grow. Like flowers. And relationships. People who are both good *and* warm draw friends like a magnet. In Jesus' case, Mary, Martha, and Lazarus were three of those friends. The two sisters knew this kind and tenderhearted man loved their brother and would want to know about his failing health. I think there's great significance in the fact that Mary and Martha's message included no request for Jesus to do anything. It simply said, "Lord, the one you love is very sick" (John 11:3). I believe the reason they didn't ask Jesus to do anything was because they knew it wasn't necessary. The Jesus they knew was so good that he didn't have to be asked.

Jesus' Return Demonstrated His Goodness

Sure enough, without being asked, Jesus decided to return to Bethany. A lot of people make a big deal out of the fact that he waited two days before leaving. But remember, we have reason to believe that Lazarus had died even before Jesus received the message. Plus, Jesus knew that the resurrection miracle he would eventually perform would pack more of a wallop if Lazarus had spent a few days in the tomb.

But where you can really see goodness in Jesus' return is in his response to a question his disciples asked in John 11:8. They said, "Only a few days ago the Jewish leaders in Judea were trying to kill you. Are you going there again?" It's kind of humorous that they phrased their question so delicately. What they probably wanted to say was "Lord, *please* don't make us go back there. It's too dangerous!"

But Jesus was never one to let danger or the threat of discomfort keep him from doing the right thing. In fact, that's how he ended up on earth in the first place! Philippians 2:6-8 says, "Though he was God, he did not demand and cling to his rights as God. He made himself nothing; he took the humble position of a slave and appeared in human form. And in human form he obediently humbled himself even further by dying a criminal's death on a cross."

I love the phrase "he made himself nothing." Do you realize how rare that is? The average person in our me-first world can't even begin to grasp the concept. We're programmed to defend our interests, fight for our rights, and pursue our own agendas—and then scream bloody murder if someone gets in our way.

But Jesus made himself *nothing.* He put other people's needs ahead of his own. He fought for other people's rights, while allowing his enemies to walk all over his. And the only agenda he ever pursued was the one that was going to open the door to Heaven for pathetic sinners like you and me.

So it isn't surprising that he would shrug off the danger involved in returning to Judea. It's the same selfless spirit that compelled a young David to do battle with an armored behemoth named Goliath. It's the same selfless spirit that compelled Shadrach, Meschach, and Abednego to stand firm in their faith, even as the flames of a hot furnace nipped at their tunics. It's the same selfless spirit that compelled Peter and John to defy the threats of the Jewish leaders and keep on preaching. And it's the same selfless spirit that compelled Stephen to ask God to forgive the bloodthirsty murderers who were stoning him.

I've always loved John 11:16. After trying, and failing, to persuade Jesus that it was too dangerous to return to Judea, Thomas spoke to the rest of the disciples and said, "Let's go, too—and die with Jesus." That statement shows that while the disciples were still very much concerned about their own interests, they were at least making progress. Selflessness wasn't their first impulse, but there was at least enough of it in them that it could be drawn out. We know that, from there, it continued to grow until it did indeed become their first impulse. History tells us that they too eventually made themselves nothing and endured unspeakable hardships for the Lord.

It's easy to see Jesus' goodness in his relationships and in his willing return to a dangerous place. But that's not all. . . .

Jesus' Response Demonstrated His Goodness

Ministers generally handle death pretty well. If you spend as much time around sick and dying people as we do, officiate enough funeral services, and counsel enough bereaved families, you eventually become pretty tough. When I first started in the ministry, I wept at every funeral and wondered if I'd ever be able to get through one without breaking down. Now, hundreds of funerals later, I have no problem keeping the tears at bay. The only exception is when a close friend dies. Then all bets are off.

One of the reasons I love the story of Lazarus's resurrection is because it shows me that Jesus had a similar experience. No one ever had more reasons to weep than he did, yet only twice do we see him doing so. He too was good at keeping the tears at bay. But when Jesus found himself standing beside the grave of one of his dearest friends, it was more than he could take. Even knowing he was going to bring Lazarus out of the tomb, his emotional dam still broke, and the tears flowed freely (John 11:35).

That's the first aspect of his response that assures me of his goodness. I love the fact that he had a tender, breakable heart . . . that he was emotionally invested in the lives of his friends. Please remember that the next time your heart is breaking. Don't assume, like so many people do, that Jesus isn't suffering right along with you. So often we conclude that because he isn't *doing* anything, he must not be *feeling* anything. But nothing could be further from the truth.

When my daughter Michelle was about two years old, she had to have some medical tests that were so unpleasant even an adult would have been tempted to sneak out the doctor's office window. The look of terror in her eyes and the bloodcurdling shrieks that exploded out of her little lungs almost did me in. My stomach felt sick, my hands were shaking, and tears filled my eyes . . . but I did nothing to stop the procedure. I know my sweet baby must have wondered at that moment why I didn't help her. I know she must have assumed her daddy didn't care. But she was wrong.

And we are wrong too when we assume that because our Lord isn't doing anything to stop our suffering, he doesn't care. The most tender verse in the Bible, "Then Jesus wept" (John 11:35), makes it clear that he feels our pain. Yes, he often allows us to go through hard times because of the benefits we gain from them. But every step of the way, he hurts right along with us.

Jesus' response to Lazarus's death wasn't just one of tears and sorrow; it was also one of action. He didn't just *feel* something; he *did* something. He raised Lazarus from the dead.

But not before uttering arguably the most encouraging words ever to fall on the human ear. In John 11:25, 26, he said, "I am the resurrection and the life. Those who believe in me, even though they die like everyone else, will live again. They are given eternal life for believing in me and will never perish."

Have you ever been in the presence of a grieving person and not known what to say? Several years ago, I walked into a woman's hospital room about five minutes after her doctor told her she had just a few months to live. Her husband was with her, and they were both weeping and holding each other. Naturally, they looked to me, their minister, for some words of encouragement. I told them what I always tell people in that situation—that I didn't have any, but Jesus did. Then I picked up the Gideon Bible on the woman's bedside table and turned to John 11:25, 26.

For people living in a world of pain and loss, these are two of the most important verses in the Bible. Years ago, an old preacher said to me, "Mark, if you're going to be a preacher, you'd better memorize John 11:25, 26. You're going to need those verses more than any others." So I did and I have. Those two verses are what you say when you don't know what to say.

And here again, we see the goodness of Jesus. His words were perfectly appropriate, tender, and hopeful. He could have told the mourners to pull themselves together. He could have said, "Martha, I'm surprised at you. I thought you had more faith than this. You need to buck up, girl." Instead, he proved himself to be the God who "comforts us in all our troubles" (2 Corinthians 1:4).

And then he got down to business.

To the burial site they all went, walking toward one of the greatest moments in history. After opening the tomb and praying, Jesus spoke three words: "Lazarus, come out!" (John 11:43). And suddenly, squinting in the sunshine, the people saw movement in the dark shadows of the cave.

It's here that we come face-to-face with the ultimate indicator of our Lord's goodness—he has made it his eternal purpose to rescue people from dark places. From tombs, yes, but also from the dark places that ensnare us when we're alive. In Luke 4:18, 19, Jesus said, "The Spirit of the Lord is upon me, for he has appointed me to preach Good News to the poor. He has sent me to proclaim that captives will be released, that the blind will see, that the downtrodden will be freed from their oppressors, and that the time of the Lord's favor has come."

Perhaps the Lord rescued you from a dark place at one time in your life. Or you may be trapped in a dark place at this very moment, wondering if it's really possible that you could finally be set free. Look at those three key words again: "Lazarus, come out!"

Now, remove Lazarus's name and insert yours.

Say it out loud.

Say it again.

Hear the Lord calling you to leave the darkness behind and step into the sunshine. He promised that captives would be released. There's no reason why you shouldn't be one of them.

I know that as long as this world keeps spinning, people will keep calling our Lord's goodness into question. And I will admit that I don't understand everything he does—or doesn't—do. But in the end, I know that he cares about what I'm going through, that he comes to me when I need him, that he feels my pain, and that, because of the gracious gift of his power, no tomb—literal or figurative—will ever be able to hold me.

That's good enough for me.

topping it off

1. *Have you ever had someone get in your face and tell you what a terrible person you are?* Detail the story and consider whether you deserved the attack.

2. *Satan knows that when that idea [that the Lord isn't as good as you thought] sinks its roots into your mind, the draining of your faith will begin in earnest. From that point on, every time something bad happens, you'll throw a suspicious glare in the Lord's direction.* Have you ever been suspicious of the Lord? Have you ever blamed him for something bad that happened? What was it? How do you feel now? If your feelings have changed, what caused that change?

3. *There are two kinds of goodness: the cold kind and the warm kind.* What kind do you have? To make sure you're seeing yourself as you really are, would you be willing to ask a few friends, family members,

classmates, or coworkers to give their opinions? What could you do to warm up your goodness even more?

4. *Jesus was never one to let danger or the threat of discomfort keep him from doing the right thing.* What about you? Does your goodness fluctuate depending on the level of discomfort you're asked to face? Reflect on a time when you did the right thing, even though you knew you'd suffer for it.

5. *Jesus' response to Lazarus's death wasn't just one of tears and sorrow; it was also one of action. He didn't just* feel *something; he* did *something.* When you encounter hurting people, how likely are you to do something? Give an example of a time when you went out of your way to minister to someone in need. Is there someone right now you can think of who needs you? What will you do?

7

REFILLING YOUR FAITH IN HIS VICTORY

JOHN 20:1-18

How we thank God, who gives us victory over sin and death through Jesus Christ our Lord!

—THE APOSTLE PAUL, 1 CORINTHIANS 15:57

Victory.

By definition, it's the defeat of an enemy or opponent. I just Googled the word and came up with 232 million hits. And yes, I counted the zeros correctly. It wasn't 232 thousand. It was 232 *million*. Everybody, it seems, wants to attach themselves to this word. Scrolling through the first few pages, I found countless things that were named Victory Something-or-other. Here are a few examples: a record company, a beer, a television show, a church, a dry cleaner, a theater, a magazine, a car dealership, a museum, a cruise ship, a nature trail, a hotel, a movie studio, and a gay and lesbian fund-raising organization.

With 232 million hits and people from all walks of life latching onto the word, we could easily conclude that victory is the most common thing in the world. That notion is reinforced when we see mob scenes on the pitcher's mound after the seventh game of the World Series, police officers cuffing and hauling away bad guys on the evening news, or entertainment celebrities hoisting little statues over their heads and making idiotic acceptance speeches.

But I suspect Solomon was closer to the truth when he said, "So what do people get for all their hard work? Their days of labor are filled with pain and grief; even at night they cannot rest. It is all utterly meaningless" (Ecclesiastes 2:22, 23). He was observing what I (and probably you) have observed: that, notwithstanding the highlight reel moments we see flashing across our TV screens every day, defeat is more common than victory. He was acknowledging that at any given moment there are more people suffering than celebrating . . . that many poor souls have given up hope of ever achieving a meaningful victory in their lives. Perhaps this is why we are so drawn to the word *victory*. People taste it so infrequently and long for it so desperately that anything connected to the word—even if the connection is dubious—is automatically elevated in our estimation.

Far too many Christians look and sound like people who've never tasted any kind of victory. Even though we are more than conquerors through Christ, who loved us (Romans 8:37, *NIV*), and even though we are not like people who have no hope (1 Thessalonians 4:13), we tend to walk around with all the mirth and optimism of a freshly neutered Chihuahua. But then again, when a person's faith reserves are depleted, I suppose it's inevitable that he would manifest such a gloomy countenance. Nothing depends on our faith more than our hope.

Right now, if you are the owner of a long face (and your name is not Jay Leno), I want to take you back to that misty morning two millennia ago when the Grim Reaper took one on the chin and went down for the count. If it's been a while since you reviewed the story in John 20, let it refill your faith, resuscitate your hope, and turn your frown upside down.

The Ultimate Victory Garden

During World War II, ordinary citizens were asked to make a contribution to the war effort in whatever way they could. Many bought bonds, saved and recycled raw materials, assisted friends and neighbors in need, and planted what came to be known as victory gardens. Urban and rural people alike planted fruits and vegetables, not only to provide for their own needs but also to ship to our troops around the world. When people spoke of the "national war effort," they were right on target. While many were fighting with guns and ammo, many more were fighting with seeds and fertilizer.

But the ultimate victory garden is the one Mary Magdalene entered with a heavy heart on the Sunday morning following Jesus' crucifixion. She hadn't just lost a friend or a loved one. She had witnessed the cruel murder of the one person who had done more for her than anyone else ever would . . . or could. Jesus had cast seven demons out of her, he had treated her with dignity and respect, he had seen her potential and cultivated it, and he had defended her when others criticized. Mary was a woman who'd grown accustomed to scorn and ridicule. At one time, she probably thought she'd never be treated with such love and kindness. And now, with Jesus dead and buried, she surely believed she never would receive such treatment again.

I'd love to know what she was thinking as she made her way along the garden path in the predawn darkness. Was she watching a movie in her mind, replaying the many unforgettable moments she'd shared with Jesus? Was she boiling with anger at the way he had been treated? Was she wondering what on earth she was going to do without her best friend? Whatever she was thinking, we know she wasn't entertaining the possibility that Jesus could be alive. Even when she saw the stone rolled away from the entrance to the tomb, not even a sprout of hope popped through the topsoil of her mind. She automatically assumed someone had stolen his body. And why wouldn't she make such an assumption? With all the other indignities Jesus had suffered, the theft of his body or the desecration of his grave would almost be expected.

Seeing the grave empty, she must have wondered who had turned grave robber . . . and why. Were Jesus' killers so twisted that they would want to put his body on display, perhaps to intimidate his followers or any other would-be messiahs? Or maybe the disciples took his body away to prevent such a scenario.

After reporting her discovery to Peter and John, Mary found herself standing outside the tomb, weeping. Suddenly, angels appeared and asked her why she was crying. Mary was answering them when she heard something behind her. Looking over her shoulder, she saw Jesus, but didn't recognize him. More than a few Bible students have wondered how that could happen.

Not me.

I've had plenty of similar incidents in my own life. For example, the other day I was in a Dillard's department store, riffling through a rack of men's dress shirts. Standing next to me was a woman I'd never seen before. Suddenly, she started talking to me as if I were her husband. She held up a shirt and said, "Oh, I like this one. It'll go with your new Dockers. But it looks a little small for a large. Do you think it'll fit?" I didn't know what to say. I knew I wasn't who she thought I was. Before I could answer, she turned and looked at me—and just about had a coronary. She apologized, slapped the shirt back onto the rack, and took off like someone fighting the effects of some bad Mexican food.

The point is, she saw me, but she didn't really *see* me. And we were in a well-lit department store, not in a misty, shadowy garden early in the morning. So I have no trouble picturing this case of mistaken identity. Mary wasn't expecting to see Jesus, so she didn't.

Until he said her name.

That moment of recognition is, to me, one of the most stirring in Scripture. If the Bible had a musical soundtrack, you can bet the violins would be swirling in a majestic crescendo at that instant when Mary's worst nightmare unexpectedly turned into her greatest joy. Many people believe (and a few manuscripts indicate) that she ran to Jesus and embraced him. I have no problem picturing that. I can see him smiling as she buried her face in his robe and held on tight. I can even imagine tears welling up in his eyes. After all he'd been through, it had to feel great to be so loved and cherished.

I'm sure Mary couldn't begin to fathom the repercussions of what she was experiencing. There's no way she could have processed all the theological implications of a living, breathing Jesus in that brief, emotionally charged moment. Nor did she have any idea of the place in history she had instantly achieved. All she knew—all she cared about—was that Jesus, her dearest friend and the kindest man she'd ever known, was alive. It wasn't until later that she began to see the big picture and grasp the significance of what had happened.

If it's been a while since you thought about Jesus' victory over death, let me remind you of three faith-filling truths.

HIS VICTORY WAS COMPLETE

Many so-called victories in this world are partial, at best. Take our invasion of Iraq, for example. Did our air and infantry forces demonstrate superiority over the enemy? Yes. Did our armored vehicles roll from the border straight into Baghdad without even tapping the brakes? Yes. Did Saddam's statue get torn down to the hoots and hollers of a grateful population? Yes. All of these things enabled us to claim victory. The problem is that we're still fighting insurgents while trying to help Iraq's infant democracy stand on its own two feet. As many pundits have observed, we won the war just fine. It's winning the peace we're struggling with.

Another example of a partial victory can be seen in a car crash victim from our area. His injuries were so extensive that he was given little chance of surviving. However, some brilliant doctors did amazing work and managed to save his life. The problem is that he has some mild brain damage and will be confined to a wheelchair for the rest of his life. So yes, in one sense, the doctors won a great victory. But they, the victim, and the victim's family will tell you that they were hoping for more.

There are many times in life when a partial victory, though

disappointing, is still better than no victory. But when it comes to any battle with death, a partial victory is not only unacceptable, it's impossible. Death has to be defeated completely or not at all, and that's what Jesus did. There are three ways in which Jesus' victory was complete.

IT RENDERED DEATH THOROUGHLY IMPOTENT

Paul said it this way: "Death is swallowed up in victory" (1 Corinthians 15:54). I can't read those words without thinking of a buddy of mine who has a pet snake. (Terrific guy, but he really needs prayer!) Every so often he feeds his snake a live rat. (Really now, don't snakes and rats deserve each other?) The snake swallows the rat whole. Nothing restricts an animal's potential like being swallowed whole by another animal. Likewise, when death was "swallowed up," it was rendered thoroughly impotent.

IT WILL NEVER HAVE TO BE WON AGAIN

Most victories are only temporary. Whoever wins the Super Bowl or the World Series this year will have to go out and compete for the championship again next year. An artist who wins the Grammy for Song of the Year this year must try to outdo himself next year. The same is true for an actor who wins a coveted Oscar. And every patient who is given a clean bill of health from his doctor today knows there will be other illnesses he'll have to contend with in the future. But never again will our Lord have to contend with sin and death. Romans 6:10 says, "He died once to defeat sin, and now he lives for the glory of God."

EVERYONE CAN HAVE ACCESS TO IT

So many things in this world are private or restricted. You can be turned away because you don't have a ticket, a membership, a reservation, an important friend, a recognizable name, the proper clothing, or a couple of C-notes to bribe the doorman. Not long ago, I showed up at a prestigious country club for a round of golf and was told that because I was wearing denim shorts, I'd have to come back some other time. But when it comes to our Lord's victory over death, there are no goons standing at the door to keep people out. Hebrews 7:25 says, "He is able, once and forever, to save *everyone* who comes to God through him." (emphasis added)

His Victory Was Conspicuous

The second great faith-filling fact about our Lord's victory over death is that it was accomplished openly, for all to see. His birth wasn't. He came into the world quietly . . . so quietly that the people staying next door at the Bethlehem Bed & Breakfast had no idea what was happening. You can also find instances in Scripture where Jesus tried to move from town to town secretly (Mark 7:24) and where he told people he had healed not to make a big deal out of his actions (Mark 8:25, 26). But his conquest of death was the centerpiece of his life's work and was put on open display. Look at this telling passage from Paul:

> I passed on to you what was most important and what had also been passed on to me—that Christ died for our sins, just as the Scriptures said. He was buried, and he was raised from the dead on the third day, as the Scriptures said. He was seen by Peter and then by the twelve apostles. After that, he was seen by more than five hundred of his followers at one time, most of whom are still alive, though some have died by now. Then he was seen by James and later by all the apostles. Last of all, I saw him, too, long after the others, as though I had been born at the wrong time (1 Corinthians 15:3-8).

The key phrase there is "most of whom are still alive." In essence, Paul was saying, "If you don't believe me, go talk to the hundreds of people who saw him with their own eyes." We might smell something fishy if all the supposed witnesses just happened to be dead. Or if there were only one or two witnesses, we might suspect some sort of bribe. But it's hard to imagine even the most resourceful person being able to enlist hundreds of people in a conspiracy.

Paul also points out that all twelve of the apostles were eyewitnesses of Christ's resurrection. Our strongest evidence that Jesus' followers weren't just fabricating a juicy story is the fact that they were willing to be persecuted and, ultimately, to die for it. Early church tradition says that Mark died in Alexandria, Egypt, after being dragged by horses through the streets. It also suggests that Luke was hanged in Greece and that Peter was crucified upside down because he didn't feel worthy to die the way Christ did. As the rows of white crosses in any military cemetery would prove, lots of people are willing to die for their heartfelt convictions. But few, if any, would knowingly die for a hoax.

Several times in my life I've chosen to accept somebody's word even though the person had no hard evidence to back up the claims. Usually, I've done this because of some emotional attachment to the person. In other words, I *wanted* to believe. But I'm forced to admit that at least half the time, my faith was misplaced and the person turned out to be less than honest. I am deeply grateful to God that he accomplished the crowning work of his redemptive plan conspicuously . . . that he gave us lots of evidence, not just to bolster our faith, but to keep us from living with the gnawing fear that we're being hoodwinked.

His Victory Is Conditional

The third great faith-filling truth about our Lord's victory over death is that any of us can share in it on one condition. That condition is clearly stated in 1 John 5:11, 12: "This is what God has testified: He has given us eternal life, and this life is in his Son. So whoever has God's Son has life; whoever does not have his Son does not have life." Peter echoed the idea in Acts 4:12. Speaking of Jesus, he said, "There is salvation in no one else! There is no other name in all of heaven for people to call on to save them."

No true Christian would ever argue this point. However, there has been much debate about the proper *way* to accept Christ. For many people, it's just a matter of believing. Others would say that faith needs to be accompanied by the sinner's prayer in order to be acknowledged and accepted by God. I must confess that I don't feel comfortable with either of these notions.

For one thing, a person can believe in God and not be obedient to him on any level. This is the point James was making when he said, "Do you still think it's enough just to believe that there is one God? Well, even the demons believe this, and they tremble in terror!" (James 2:19). Clearly, James says, no one believes more than Satan and his minions . . . but they are not saved. Yes, I know John 3:16 and several other verses talk about believing and being saved. But the wise Bible student always allows one verse to shed light on another. If James 2:19 is true, then there can be no such thing as "faith only" salvation.

I also have a problem with what's commonly referred to as the sinner's prayer. The Bible does say that "anyone who calls on the name of the Lord will be saved" (Romans 10:13). But when Paul said that, did he really intend for us to come up with a special prayer to be parroted like some sort of incantation by every person who wants to be a Christian? And if he did, why don't the conversion accounts in Scripture feature such a recitation? When Peter concluded his Day of Pentecost sermon in Acts 2, why didn't he ask the three thousand people in the audience who wanted to be saved simply to bow their heads and repeat the sinner's prayer? He could have done exactly that. Without question, it would have been easier than having all those people parade down to the local watering hole to be baptized.

Please understand, I'm not challenging the faith or sincerity of any person who's ever recited the sinner's prayer. If you did, don't panic. All I ask is that you look beyond the sinner's prayer and see what people in the Bible *really* did when they accepted Christ. I see five things.

They believed

In the book of Acts, where many conversion stories are documented, the word *believed* is used eighteen times in some sort of statement about salvation. Acts 5:14, for example, says, "More and more people believed and were brought to the Lord—crowds of both men and women."

They changed

In Colossians 1:6, Paul said, "This same Good News that came to you is going out all over the world. It is changing lives everywhere, just as it changed yours that very first day you heard and understood the truth about God's great kindness to sinners." He said it even more forcefully in Galatians 6:15: "What counts is whether we really have been changed into new and different people."

This side of Heaven we will never attain perfection. Spiritual growth is a lifelong process that will always have its ups and downs, but the journey has to start somewhere. In Luke 13:3 Jesus admonished us to "turn from [our] evil ways and turn to God." He left no wiggle room. He saw this life change as a requirement to be met, not an option to be considered.

They spoke openly about their allegiance to Christ

Even when they were being persecuted, they courageously testified of their faith.

On one occasion, Peter and John were ordered by the religious power brokers never to speak or teach about Jesus again. They responded with one of the most inspirational statements in Scripture when they said, "Do you think God wants us to obey you rather than him? We cannot stop telling about the wonderful things we have seen and heard" (Acts 4:19, 20).

Peter viewed his witnessing as an act of obedience to God. No doubt, the words of Jesus were ringing in his ears. In Matthew 10:32, 33, he said, "If anyone acknowledges me publicly here on earth, I will openly acknowledge that person before my Father in heaven. But if anyone denies me here on earth, I will deny that person before my Father in heaven." Later, Paul reiterated the importance of confessing Christ when he said, "It is by believing in your heart that you are made right with God, and it is by confessing with your mouth that you are saved" (Romans 10:10). Again, with such powerful, unequivocal statements on the subject, it's hard to see how openly confessing one's allegiance to Christ could be considered optional.

THEY WERE IMMERSED

A lot of people feel uncomfortable connecting baptism to salvation. They say it's a work and that salvation is by grace, not works. Rather than quibbling over such matters, I prefer to look at the big picture. Baptism was commanded (Acts 2:38; 22:16), baptism was practiced (Acts 2:41), and baptism was connected to salvation, according to the Bible writers. Acts 2:38 specifically says that baptism should be "in the name of Jesus Christ for the forgiveness of your sins," and 1 Peter 3:21 says that baptism "saves you by the power of Jesus Christ's resurrection." I suppose the fuss over baptism's significance will continue until the Lord returns, but I've never understood it. I think it would be easier to climb Mt. Everest barefooted than to explain why baptism isn't important.

THEY PERSEVERED IN THE FAITH

In those early days of the church, Christians were told to expect persecution and to endure it with a good attitude (1 Peter 4:12, 13). They were also told that their salvation depended on their ability to do so. John said, "You must remain faithful to what you have been taught from the beginning. If you do, you will continue to live in fellowship with the Son and with the Father. And in this fellowship we enjoy the eternal life he promised us" (1 John 2:24, 25).

And with that statement, we come full circle . . . back to the victory over death that Jesus won and now offers to us.

Paul says in Romans 8:37 that "overwhelming victory is ours through Christ, who loved us." The word "overwhelming" makes all the difference. It reminds me that the words *barely, close call,* or *by the skin of your teeth* do not apply to my victory in Christ. This is what enables me to relax and enjoy the ride. So many Christians seem to be afraid that they're going to squeak into Heaven under the wire, if at all. Just ask the next Christian you see if he's going to Heaven. There's a good chance he'll shrug and meekly say "I hope so."

Not me.

I believe my victory is overwhelming.

But not because of me.

My victory is overwhelming because of Jesus. Who he is and what he did. It's *all* overwhelming.

So how could my victory in him be any less?

topping it off

1. *All she knew—all she cared about—was that Jesus, her dearest friend and the kindest man she'd ever known, was alive. It wasn't until later that she began to see the big picture and grasp the significance of what had happened.* Think about your conversion experience. How much did you really understand when you first claimed Christ's victory? What are some truths you began to grasp later? Are you still growing in your appreciation of what he did for you?

2. *There are many times in life when a partial victory, though disappointing, is still better than no victory.* Can you point to an example of this in your own life? Why was your victory in this area not complete? Has anything changed that might enable you to try again and gain a complete victory?

3. *I am deeply grateful to God that he accomplished the crowning work of his redemptive plan conspicuously . . . that he gave us lots of evidence, not just to bolster our faith, but to keep us from living with the gnawing fear that we're being hoodwinked.* Have you ever been afraid, even momentarily, that Christianity was the ultimate snipe hunt and that you were the butt of the joke? If so, what triggered that fear? How did you deal with it? What facts give you the most assurance that the gospel is true?

4. *Spiritual growth is a lifelong process that will always have its ups and downs, but the journey has to start somewhere.* When you accepted Christ, did anyone explain why it's so important to change your lifestyle? What changes can you point to in your life that are the direct result of your commitment to Christ? Are there other changes you need to make?

8
REFILLING YOUR FAITH
IN HIS RETURN

MATTHEW 24:36-51

He who loves the coming of the Lord is not he who affirms it is far off, nor is it he who says it is near. It is he, who, whether it be far or near, awaits it with sincere faith, steadfast hope, and fervent love.

—AUGUSTINE

I am terrible at math. When I was in high school, I made it through algebra and geometry only because the teacher liked me. When my daughter, who is also mathematically challenged, was in high school, I couldn't even help her with her homework. My best advice to her was, "Just be really nice and polite to your teacher. Maybe she'll cut you some slack."

At least I'm not alone.

Perhaps the largest demographic group in America is that collection of people who couldn't work an algebra problem if their lives depended on it. The thing that marks us is that we stand in awe of anyone who's good with numbers. While others admire the world's great military leaders and Nobel Prize winners, our heroes are those people who can look at their restaurant bills and calculate a 15 percent tip in their heads.

This explains Edgar Whisenant.[1]

He was a NASA rocket scientist—the kind of guy who would have aced calculus and trig—which tells you right away that a huge segment of the American population thought he was some kind of god. After all, we often say, "You don't have to be a rocket scientist to know that." Obviously, we think rocket scientists set the standard for intelligence (because, after all, nothing has *ever* gone wrong at NASA, right?).

Well, Edgar was an honest-to-goodness rocket scientist, so immediately he got a free pass. People figured somebody that smart couldn't possibly do something really dumb. So when he wrote a booklet called *88 Reasons Why the Rapture Could Be in 1988*, people ate it up to the tune of four million copies sold. In the booklet, he claimed that the rapture would happen between September 11 and 13, 1988, and that the only way he could be wrong would be if the Bible were in error. You can imagine the hullabaloo when September 14 arrived and everybody still seemed to be present and accounted for.

Good ol' Edgar, not to be thwarted, sharpened his pencil and reapplied those impressive math skills. And wouldn't you know . . . he found a mistake! It wasn't September 11 or 13; it was September 15! After slapping his forehead and saying, "Duh!" he announced to the world that Christians everywhere ought to lace up their sneakers real tight lest they be sucked right out of them at the big moment.

But again, nothing happened.

So Edgar pushed the date to October 3.

And again, nothing happened.

This is about the time Edgar's little booklet started being used as a coaster in homes all across America.

But if you think Edgar Whisenant's buffoonery is the weirdest thing to come out of man's obsession with the end times, think again. Even Edgar can't top the geniuses who identified Barney, the purple dinosaur, as the Antichrist.

What? You didn't know Barney is the Antichrist? Then you need to read Revelation 13:18. It clearly says that the beast's number is

666, which also happens to be Barney's number. If you have any doubts, just work through the following steps and be enlightened:

> Given: Barney is a cute purple dinosaur
> Prove: Barney is really the Antichrist in disguise
> 1. Start with the given: CUTE PURPLE DINOSAUR
> 2. Change all the U's to V's (which is proper Latin anyway): CVTE PVRPLE DINOSAVR
> 3. Extract all Roman numerals in the phrase: CVVLDIV
> 4. Convert these into Arabic values: 100 5 5 50 500 1 5
> 5. Add all the numbers: 666[2]

I know what you just read seems like a joke, but there are actually people who spend their lives figuring these things out. And they're not just fooling around. They're seriously trying to unlock the mysteries of God. Honestly, I don't think any area of theology has gone quite as bonkers as eschatology, which is the study of things relating to the end times. No other area of study has produced a longer line of crackpots or a larger collection of goofy math exercises.

But I guess we shouldn't be surprised. The public has an insatiable hunger for all things eschatological, as evidenced by the mind-boggling popularity of the Left Behind series, authored by Tim LaHaye and Jerry Jenkins. When all is said and done, there will be twelve novels, three prequels, and one sequel. The authors initially had no intention of writing that many, but when the first few became mega best sellers, they quickly revised their plans and stretched their story. Sadly, people who've never read one word of the Bible have read every Left Behind novel and think, therefore, that they have a clear understanding of how the world's going to end.

We need to be wary of any person who claims to know exactly what's going to happen. So much of God's plan regarding the end of the world is shrouded in mystery. And it doesn't matter what position you take on a given issue, there's almost always an alternative view that makes at least some sense.

Let me give you an example.

The LaHaye/Jenkins view of the end of the world hinges on the rapture, which finds its scriptural roots in Matthew 24:40, 41: "Two men will be working together in the field; one will be taken, the other left. Two women will be grinding flour at the mill; one will be taken, the other left. So be prepared, because you don't know what day your Lord is coming."

People who believe in the rapture will tell you that it's the good guys who will be taken and the bad guys who will be left behind. But where does it say that? As far as I can see, Jesus doesn't say which group will be taken and which group will be left.

There are, however, some indications in Scripture that the *bad* guys might be taken and the *good* guys left behind. For example, Jesus told a parable about a farmer who had a wheat field. During the night, his enemy came and planted weeds among the wheat. Before long, the weeds grew up and choked the wheat, so the farmer's servants begged for permission to take action. But the farmer refused to give it. Instead, he promised that, at harvest time, the weeds (bad guys) would be—*not* left behind—but pulled out, taken way, and burned (Matthew 13:24-30).

I'm not taking either of these positions. And I think Jesus is making an entirely different point in that section of Matthew 24. I'm merely pointing out that even the most popular notions regarding the end of the world can be challenged. Therefore, anybody who claims to have it all figured out is someone whose views you probably want to approach with caution.

The only thing we can really be sure of is that Jesus is indeed coming again.

Or is he?

Do you ever wonder?

In his book *The Second Coming*, John MacArthur mentions a survey of Protestant ministers that was taken at a church convention in Evanston, Illinois. Ninety percent said they had no expectation whatsoever that Christ would ever really return to earth.[3] Those skeptics would likely tell you that Jesus' words regarding his return to earth were twisted and embellished by those who wrote them down . . . that he never actually said he was coming back. Or they might try to spiritualize his return, saying that it happens in an individual's heart when he accepts the Lord.

But what's just as disturbing as those who reject a literal second coming is the startling number of believers who don't seem to be living with the expectation of it happening anytime soon. As I was writing this book, I asked Christians across denominational lines to share their thoughts on the second coming; and while I couldn't find anyone who would flat-out say he didn't believe in it, I also couldn't find anyone who was excited about it or who even thought about it very often. One lady seemed to be speaking for the group when she shrugged and said, "It's not something that's on my mind. I guess it should be, but it isn't."

What about you?

Is the second coming anything more to you than a plotline for a series of novels? Do you truly believe that before you finish reading this chapter, Christ could appear and usher in the fulfillment of God's redemptive plan? And have you built your life on that possibility? Can you honestly say that your life is in order, that you've made all the necessary preparations, and that you'd be ready to welcome him without fear or embarrassment? Do you think about his coming and hope for it every day?

If not, it's high time you gave our Lord's return some serious thought because the clock *is* ticking.

What Jesus Wants You to Know

Matthew 24 is where most people start building their end-times theology. Bible students fuss and argue about which of Jesus' remarks refer to the destruction of the Jerusalem temple (which occurred in 70 AD) and which refer to his second coming. I can assure you that far more intelligent people than I have already plowed that ground, so I don't intend to do it again. What I want to focus on are three unmistakable truths that come blazing through the fog like lasers.

Jesus is coming back

Jesus begins Matthew 24:37 by saying, "When the Son of Man returns. . . ." Not *if* he returns, but "when" he returns.

In John 14:3, he also made it crystal clear. At a time when the disciples were worried about how they were going to get along without him, Jesus gave them hope by saying, "When everything is ready, I will come and get you, so that you will always be with me where I am." Many aspects of end-times theology are debatable, but not our Lord's promise to return.

What he *doesn't* tell us is *when* he's coming back. And if you think about it, that makes perfect sense. Allow me to illustrate in a way that I'm sure will dredge up unpleasant memories in the minds of some of my church members.

Poinciana Christian Church's facility is located on a busy highway in central Florida, a highway that is notorious for its speeders. Every now and then, the Osceola County Sheriff's Department sets up a speed trap. They have two or three perfect little hiding places, and they nail car after car after car.

But they have never nailed me.

Not because I am such an angel behind the wheel. Oh no! The reason they have never caught me is because I know from years of observation how unpredictable they are. They show up on different days and at different times so that you can never anticipate when they might be there. So the only way to keep from getting a ticket is to obey the speed limit *all* the time. Trust me. If I knew ahead of time when they were and were not going to be out there with their little radar guns, I'd be tempted to adjust my speed accordingly.

Likewise, not knowing when Jesus is going to show up motivates people to get (and keep) their lives in order. Recently, a man told me that he broke off an illicit sexual affair because he heard a sermon about the Lord returning unexpectedly and catching people in compromising situations that would likely cost them their souls. The man said that the next time he was with the woman, it was all he could think about. Fear and guilt pressed on his chest like an anvil, and he ended the relationship the next day.

This is what the Edgar Whisenants of this world have never figured out. They sit around with their calendars and slide rules, chicken-scratching their calculations, narrowing down the possible dates of our Lord's return—and apparently never stop to think that God has good reasons for not allowing that mystery to be solved.

MANY PEOPLE WON'T BE READY WHEN HE RETURNS

Jesus says, "When the Son of Man returns, it will be like it was in Noah's day. In those days before the Flood, the people were enjoying banquets and parties and weddings right up to the time Noah entered his boat. People didn't realize what was going to happen until the Flood came and swept them all away. That is the way it will be when the Son of Man comes" (Matthew 24:37-39).

Many people think of "Noah's day" as a time of decadence, and it was. But that doesn't seem to be Jesus' emphasis here. If he wanted to paint a picture of a world gone wild, he surely would have come up with some more striking terminology. "Enjoying banquets and parties and weddings" doesn't exactly conjure up visions of drunken multitudes carousing on Bourbon Street during Mardi Gras. We've all been to banquets, parties, and weddings where no one danced on the table with a lamp shade on his head.

Jesus' point seems to be that *good* people are going to be preoccupied and, therefore, unprepared for his return—which makes the informal survey I mentioned a moment ago very unnerving. Again, the thing I heard from most of the people I spoke to is that they rarely think about the second coming. What they *do* think about is making the mortgage payment, picking up the dry cleaning, and getting the kids to their piano lessons on time. As one person recently said to me, "I want to do more for God, but *life* keeps getting in my way!"

NOBODY HAS TO BE CAUGHT UNPREPARED FOR HIS RETURN

When someone has a powerful point to make, he'll state it and then illustrate it. And if he really wants to drive the point home, he'll illustrate it twice. In chapters 24 and 25 of Matthew, Jesus talks about the importance of being ready at all times for his coming, and then he drives the point home with a whopping six illustrations:

- A homeowner and a thief (24:43, 44)
- A faithful servant (24:45-47)
- An unfaithful servant (24:48-51)
- Ten bridesmaids (25:1-13)
- Servants left in charge of their master's resources (25:14-30)
- The dividing of the sheep and the goats (25:31-46)

No other place in Scripture will you find Jesus using six consecutive illustrations to drive home a point. That fact alone tells you that he considers this message to be of vital importance.

He's coming back.

Most people won't be ready.

But you *can* be.

That's what Jesus wants you to know.

What Jesus Wants You to Remember

As you read the New Testament, you notice that its writers believed the Lord was going to return very soon. The following verses serve as good examples of their thriving sense of anticipation:

- "Another reason for right living is that you know how late it is; time is running out. Wake up, for the coming of our salvation is nearer now than when we first believed. The night is almost gone; the day of salvation will soon be here" (Romans 13:11, 12).
- "The God of peace will soon crush Satan under your feet" (Romans 16:20).
- "Let us not neglect our meeting together, as some people do, but encourage and warn each other, especially now that the day of his coming back again is drawing near" (Hebrews 10:25).
- "In just a little while, the Coming One will come and not delay" (Hebrews 10:37).
- "The end of the world is coming soon. Therefore, be earnest and disciplined in your prayers" (1 Peter 4:7).
- "Dear children, the last hour is here. You have heard that the Antichrist is coming, and already many such antichrists have appeared. From this we know that the end of the world has come" (1 John 2:18).

Yet, in spite of their belief that Jesus' return was right around the corner, here we sit almost two millennia later, still waiting. It's enough to make even the most dedicated believer wonder if (a) the Bible writers knew what they were talking about, or (b) the Lord has changed his mind about coming back.

Adding to our confusion is the chorus of skeptics who never

miss an opportunity to make light of our Lord's delay. Second Peter 3:3, 4 says, "I want to remind you that in the last days there will be scoffers who will laugh at the truth and do every evil thing they desire. This will be their argument: 'Jesus promised to come back, did he? Then where is he?'" Perhaps you've had an unbelieving coworker or family member ask you that very question while wearing a smug little smirk.

I believe Jesus would want you simply to remember three faith-filling facts.

He has never, ever lied

You can't point to one thing Jesus ever said and say "That wasn't true." In fact, Jesus was so committed to the truth that he told it even when he knew it would cause him great suffering.

Consider his many run-ins with the Jewish leaders. He knew they hated him and wanted to see him dead. He knew they were looking for any excuse to have him arrested. In a similar situation, you and I would, at the very least, keep our mouths shut. More likely, we would say what was politically correct even if we didn't really believe it, just to keep our heads out of a noose. But Jesus spoke the pure, unadulterated truth. He looked those egomaniacs in the eye and said, "You reject God's laws in order to hold on to your own traditions" (Mark 7:9).

If Jesus had had an agent, a publicist, or a group of handlers like so many modern evangelists, they would have ushered him aside and cautioned him: "Look, you can't be saying things like that. It's not good for business. Even if you can't stand these people, you need to smile and act sociable. Remember, the point is to draw people in, not drive them away."

But Jesus could no more put on an act than an elephant could perform ballet. He spoke the truth because he was (and is) the truth (John 14:6).

Does it stand to reason that Jesus would tell the truth about everything else and then lie about his return?

He hates evil and injustice

We tend to think of Jesus as being gentle, meek, and mild. But there were times when he got riled up, and those times were always when he was confronted with evil. The most striking example is when he walked into the outer court of the temple and saw that the money changers and animal vendors were ripping off worshipers who needed sacrifices to offer and had no choice but to pay their exorbitant prices. John 2:15 says, "Jesus made a whip from some ropes and chased them all out of the Temple." It also records the fact that he scattered their money all over the floor and turned over their tables.

I find the image of Jesus making a whip very unsettling. The Old West equivalent would be a town marshal stuffing shells into a shotgun. The modern-day equivalent would be a SWAT team member pulling on a bulletproof vest and checking the ammo in his pistol. In each scenario, you just know rear ends are about to get kicked.

Jesus' temper also flared in Mark 8 when he was talking to his disciples about his death. Peter took him aside (boy, did he have some gall!) and told Jesus he shouldn't talk like that. Jesus not only rebuked Peter, but did so "very sternly" and even called him "Satan" (vv. 32, 33).

Nothing infuriates our Lord more than an attempt to subvert his plan, whether obvious or subtle. So do you really think he would pass up an opportunity to crush all such efforts once and for all? According to Scripture, that's one of the biggest things that's going to happen at the second coming. All the forces of darkness that have been opposing God and afflicting people for millennia are going to get drop-kicked into the lake of fire (Revelation 20:15).

Does it stand to reason that Jesus would hate evil and injustice so much and then allow Satan and his minions to get off the hook in the end?

He has given his all for you

Can you imagine a young law student spending a fortune on his education, slaving through years of school, keeping inhuman hours, and meeting impossible demands—only to decide on the evening before his bar exam that he doesn't want to be an attorney after all? Nor can I. The very idea of working so hard and paying such a high price . . . of working your way to the very brink of victory and then not following through and finishing off the task is unthinkable. Yet, that's exactly what Jesus would be doing if he decided not to fulfill his promise to return.

First Thessalonians 4:16, 17 says, "The Lord himself will come down from heaven with a commanding shout, with the call of the archangel, and with the trumpet call of God. First, all the Christians who have died will rise from their graves. Then, together with them, we who are still alive and remain on the earth will be caught up in the clouds to meet the Lord in the air and remain with him forever."

And then I love the next line.

Paul says in verse 18, "So comfort and encourage each other with these words." You see, our Lord knows that the promise of his return is our hope. On the hardest of days, during the darkest of times, when we are hard-pressed to take another step, it's knowing that someday everything will be made right that keeps us going. For Jesus to renege on that promise would make him more than a liar. It would make him unspeakably cruel.

Does it stand to reason that Jesus would come so far and accomplish so much and then not finish the job?

"The Lord isn't really being slow about his promise to return, as some people think. No, he is being patient for your sake. He does not want anyone to perish, so he is giving more time for everyone to repent" (2 Peter 3:9).

We can speculate all we want about the Lord's return—when or if it's going to happen—but in the end, the answer is what it always is with Jesus.

Love.

It's what brought him to earth.

It's what put him on a cross.

It's why he's resisted every impulse to come back and clean house.

There must be somebody who isn't ready yet.

Is it you?

topping it off

1. *Edgar [Whisenant] was an honest-to-goodness rocket scientist, so immediately he got a free pass. People figured somebody that smart couldn't possibly do something really dumb.* Have you ever put your faith in someone simply because he or she was smarter than you—and then been disappointed? In the past, have you worried when you've heard predictions regarding the end of the world? What will be your attitude toward such things in the future?

2. *Sadly, people who've never read one word of the Bible have read every Left Behind novel and think, therefore, that they have a clear understanding of how the world's going to end.* Are you one of those people who will read a religious novel but not the Bible? What are the dangers in that? Do you think it's important to know the theological biases of a fiction writer before you read his or her work?

138

3. *Jesus' point seems to be that good people are going to be preoccupied and, therefore, unprepared for his return.* What evidence can you point to that would indicate your readiness to meet the Lord? Is there anything you need to do but haven't done?

4. *I find the image of Jesus making a whip very unsettling.* How often do you think about the anger of Jesus? To what extent does it motivate you to be a better Christian? Do you think it's good to be motivated by fear?

5. *Love. It's what brought him to earth. It's what put him on a cross. It's why he's resisted every impulse to come back and clean house. There must be somebody who isn't ready yet. Is it you?* Well, is it?

acknowledgments

I remember when my dream of becoming an author was on life support. After trying (and failing) to get published for eighteen years, I figured I had a better chance of becoming a prima ballerina. So you can imagine how grateful I am as this, my sixth book, sits on bookstore shelves around the world. The following people have helped me in important ways and continue to lend their support and inspiration:

My wife, Marilyn. After more than thirty years of marriage, I still have a hard time believing I found someone so wonderful . . . and that she would have me. As the saying goes, I married up. Way up.

My agent, Lee Hough, of Alive Communications. Our relationship started out as a business arrangement and quickly evolved into a friendship. Lee not only represents me with integrity and class, he enriches my life and makes me a better man.

My editors, Dale Reeves and Lynn Pratt, at Standard Publishing. I am honored to have written this book for a company that has been impacting the body of Christ for more than 135 years. Dale and Lynn are real pros who made the experience a pleasant one.

My friend, Karen Kingsbury. If you've read her books, you know what a great writer she is, but she's an even better person. She believed in me and went out of her way, far above and beyond the call of duty, to help me get published.

And to my readers: Thank you for buying and reading my books and for the wonderful e-mails you send. You have no idea what they mean to me. You can reach me at MarkAtteberry@aol.com.

notes

CHAPTER 2

1. Information in this section from www.goldenpalaceevents.com/auctions/jesuspierogi01.php (accessed November 11, 2005).

2. Albert Einstein. www.wisdomquotes.com/cat_stupidity.html (accessed May 9, 2006).

3. www.phobialist.com (accessed November 18, 2005).

4. Ron Mehl, *Surprise Endings* (Sisters, OR: Multnomah Books, 1993), 57.

CHAPTER 3

1. Information in this section from John Douglas and Stephen Singular, *Anyone You Want Me to Be* (New York: Simon & Schuster, Inc., 2003), 112–201.

2. Information in this section compiled from http://www.cbsnews.com/stories/2005/03/14/national/main679837.shtml and http://www.beliefnet.com/story/177/story_17749_1.html.

CHAPTER 4

1. Information in this section from http://www.menswearhouse.com/home_page/our_company/co611_70timeline.jsp?bmUID=1149609093854.

2. Ray Comfort, *What Hollywood Believes: An Intimate Look at the Faith of the Famous* (Bartlesville, OK: Genesis Publishing Group, 2004), 20–21.

3. Ibid., 54.

4. Ibid., 121.

CHAPTER 5

1. Leonardo da Vinci. www.brainyquote.com/quotes/authors/
l/leonardo_da_vinci.html.

2. Alan D. Wright, *Lover of My Soul* (Sisters, OR: Multnomah
Publishers, Inc., 1998), 39–40.

CHAPTER 6

1. Darrell L. Bock, *Jesus According to Scripture: Restoring the
Portrait from the Gospels* (Grand Rapids, MI: Baker Book House
Company, 2002), 478.

CHAPTER 8

1. Information in this section from Jason Boyett, *Pocket Guide
to the Apocalypse: The Official Field Manual for the End of the World*
(Orlando, FL: Relevant Books, 2005), 60–61.

2. Robert G. Clouse, Robert N. Hosack, and Richard V.
Pierard, *The New Millenium Manual: A Once and Future Guide*
(Grand Rapids, MI: Baker Book House Company, 1999), 171.

3. John F. MacArthur, *The Second Coming* (Wheaton, IL: Good
News Publishers, 1999), 27.

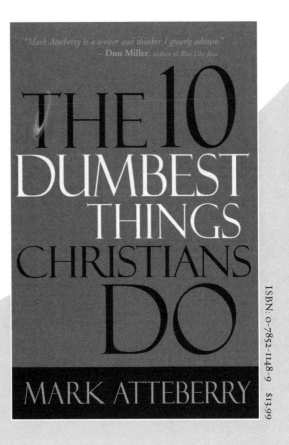